AFFILIATE MARKETING FOR BEGINNERS 2023

A New step-by-step Guide to Creating a Passive Income Stream and Mastering the World of Affiliate Marketing.

D1525515

no scenarios in which the publisher or the original author of this work can be in any fashion deemed liable for any hardship or damages that may befall them after undertaking information described herein.

Additionally, the information in the following pages is intended only for informational purposes and should thus be thought of as universal. As befitting its nature, it is presented without assurance regarding its prolonged validity or interim quality. Trademarks that are mentioned are done without written consent and can in no way be considered an endorsement from the trademark holder.

CHAPTER 1: INTRODUCTION TO AFFILIATE MARKETING 10

1.1 DEFINING AFFILIATE MARKETING 10
1.2 HISTORY AND EVOLUTION OF AFFILIATE MARKETING 11
1.3 IMPORTANCE OF AFFILIATE MARKETING IN TODAY'S DIGITAL WORLD 14
1.4 ADVANTAGES AND DISADVANTAGES OF AFFILIATE MARKETING 18

CHAPTER 2: UNDERSTANDING THE AFFILIATE MARKETING ECOSYSTEM 22

2.1 THE KEY PLAYERS: MERCHANTS, NETWORKS, PUBLISHERS, AND CUSTOMERS 22
2.2 ROLE OF AFFILIATE NETWORKS 25
2.3 THE AFFILIATE MARKETING VALUE CHAIN 27
2.4 THE LIFE CYCLE OF AN AFFILIATE MARKETING CAMPAIGN 30

CHAPTER 3: DIVING INTO INTERNET MARKETING 34

3.1 OVERVIEW OF INTERNET MARKETING 34
3.2 SEO BASICS AND IMPORTANCE IN AFFILIATE MARKETING 37
3.3 UNDERSTANDING PAY-PER-CLICK ADVERTISING 40
3.4 THE ROLE OF CONTENT MARKETING 42

CHAPTER 4: BUILDING YOUR PLATFORM 45

4.1 UNDERSTANDING YOUR PLATFORM OPTIONS 45
4.2 BUILDING YOUR OWN WEBSITE: TIPS AND STRATEGIES 47
4.3 LEVERAGING SOCIAL MEDIA FOR AFFILIATE MARKETING 50
4.4 EMAIL MARKETING AS AN AFFILIATE TOOL 53

CHAPTER 5: NICHE SELECTION FOR AFFILIATE MARKETING 56

5.1 THE IMPORTANCE OF CHOOSING A NICHE 56
5.2 RESEARCHING AND IDENTIFYING PROFITABLE NICHES 58
5.3 EVALUATING NICHE COMPETITION 60
5.4 COMMITTING TO AND DEVELOPING YOUR NICHE 63

CHAPTER 6: SELECTING THE RIGHT AFFILIATE PROGRAMS 66

6.1 CRITERIA FOR CHOOSING AFFILIATE PROGRAMS 66
6.2 UNDERSTANDING COMMISSION STRUCTURES 68
6.3 REVIEWING THE PRODUCT OR SERVICE 70
6.4 CONSIDERING AFFILIATE PROGRAM SUPPORT AND RESOURCES 72

CHAPTER 7: BUILDING TRUST AND CREDIBILITY 75

7.1 THE IMPORTANCE OF TRANSPARENCY AND HONESTY 75

7.2 BUILDING A PERSONAL BRAND 77

7.3 CREATING VALUABLE AND RELEVANT CONTENT 80

7.4 ENGAGING WITH YOUR AUDIENCE 82

CHAPTER 8: DRIVING TRAFFIC TO YOUR AFFILIATE LINKS 86

8.1 SEO STRATEGIES FOR DRIVING TRAFFIC 86

8.2 USING SOCIAL MEDIA FOR TRAFFIC GENERATION 89

8.3 PAY-PER-CLICK ADVERTISING FOR AFFILIATES 91

8.4 GUEST BLOGGING AND OTHER STRATEGIES 94

CHAPTER 9: CONVERTING TRAFFIC INTO SALES 97

9.1 UNDERSTANDING CONVERSION RATE OPTIMIZATION 97

9.2 CRAFTING EFFECTIVE CALLS TO ACTION 99

9.3 CREATING LANDING PAGES THAT CONVERT 102

9.4 TESTING AND OPTIMIZING FOR CONVERSIONS 104

CHAPTER 10: ADVANCED AFFILIATE MARKETING STRATEGIES 107

10.1 IMPLEMENTING SALES FUNNELS IN AFFILIATE MARKETING 107

10.2 RETARGETING STRATEGIES FOR AFFILIATES 109

10.3 AUTOMATING YOUR AFFILIATE MARKETING BUSINESS 112

10.4 EXPLORING MULTI-TIER AFFILIATE MARKETING 114

CHAPTER 11: MANAGING AND TRACKING YOUR AFFILIATE BUSINESS 117

11.1 TOOLS AND TECHNIQUES FOR TRACKING SUCCESS 117

11.2 INTERPRETING AND ANALYZING PERFORMANCE DATA 119

11.3 ADJUSTING STRATEGIES BASED ON PERFORMANCE 122

11.4 MANAGING MULTIPLE AFFILIATE PROGRAMS 124

CHAPTER 12: LEGAL CONSIDERATIONS AND ETHICS IN AFFILIATE MARKETING
.... 127

12.1 UNDERSTANDING LEGAL OBLIGATIONS 127

12.2 FOLLOWING FTC GUIDELINES FOR AFFILIATES 129

12.3 ETHICAL CONSIDERATIONS IN AFFILIATE MARKETING 132

12.4 MANAGING DISPUTES AND ISSUES 134

CHAPTER 13: AFFILIATE MARKETING ON DIFFERENT PLATFORMS 138

13.1 AFFILIATE MARKETING ON BLOGS 138

13.2 UTILIZING YOUTUBE FOR AFFILIATE MARKETING 141

13.3 LEVERAGING INSTAGRAM FOR AFFILIATE PROFITS 144
13.4 OTHER PLATFORMS: TIKTOK, LINKEDIN, PODCASTS 147

CHAPTER 14: SCALING YOUR AFFILIATE MARKETING BUSINESS.................... 150

14.1 OUTSOURCING TASKS AND PROCESSES 150
14.2 INVESTING IN YOUR AFFILIATE BUSINESS...153
14.3 EXPANDING INTO NEW NICHES OR MARKETS......................................156
14.4 CONSIDERING OTHER MONETIZATION STRATEGIES 158

CHAPTER 15: AFFILIATE MARKETING MISTAKES TO AVOID 161

15.1 COMMON PITFALLS FOR BEGINNERS 161
15.2 AVOIDING SCAMS AND SHADY PROGRAMS...164
15.3 BALANCING PROMOTIONAL AND NON-PROMOTIONAL CONTENT...........................167
15.4 NEGLECTING SEO AND USER EXPERIENCE 171

CHAPTER 16: CASE STUDIES OF SUCCESSFUL AFFILIATE MARKETERS 175

16.1 ANALYZING SUCCESSFUL AFFILIATE WEBSITES....................................175
16.2 INTERVIEWS WITH SUCCESSFUL AFFILIATE MARKETERS 178
16.3 LESSONS LEARNED FROM SUCCESS STORIES 181
16.4 APPLYING CASE STUDY INSIGHTS TO YOUR BUSINESS..........................185

CHAPTER 17: THE FUTURE OF AFFILIATE MARKETING...................................... 189

17.1 TRENDS IMPACTING THE AFFILIATE MARKETING INDUSTRY 189
17.2 TECHNOLOGICAL INNOVATIONS AFFECTING AFFILIATE MARKETING 193
17.3 PREDICTIONS FOR AFFILIATE MARKETING IN THE NEXT DECADE...........................197
17.4 ADAPTING TO CHANGE IN THE AFFILIATE INDUSTRY...........................201

CHAPTER 18: GETTING STARTED: YOUR FIRST 90 DAYS IN AFFILIATE MARKETING
.. 206

18.1 CREATING YOUR AFFILIATE MARKETING PLAN....................................206
18.2 SETTING UP YOUR AFFILIATE MARKETING ASSETS 210
18.3 LAUNCHING YOUR FIRST AFFILIATE MARKETING CAMPAIGN 214
18.4 EVALUATING AND ADJUSTING YOUR PLAN AFTER 90 DAYS....................218

CHAPTER 19: CONCLUSION 223

1.1 DEFINING AFFILIATE MARKETING

Affiliate marketing is a performance-based online business model in which a company, often referred to as the 'merchant' or 'advertiser', pays commissions to other parties, the 'affiliates', for referring new business to the company's website. The affiliates, also sometimes known as publishers, promote products or services offered by the merchant on their own platforms - this could be a blog, a website, a YouTube channel, or a social media account, among others. The unique element of affiliate marketing lies in its payment model. Unlike traditional advertising, where the advertiser pays for the display of ads irrespective of the results, in affiliate marketing, the merchant pays the affiliate only when a specific action takes place. These actions could range from a customer clicking on an affiliate link (Pay Per Click or PPC), signing up for a newsletter (Pay Per Lead or PPL), or making a purchase (Pay Per Sale or PPS). This way, affiliate marketing offers a win-win scenario for both merchants and affiliates. For the merchants, it is a way to reach wider audiences and increase their sales with minimal risk, as they pay only for results. For affiliates, it provides an opportunity to earn income by promoting products or services they believe in, without the need to develop products or services of their own. In this book, we will delve deeper into the specifics of affiliate marketing, explaining its inner workings, and providing practical advice for those who are interested in starting their own affiliate marketing journey.

1.2 HISTORY AND EVOLUTION OF AFFILIATE MARKETING

The concept of affiliate marketing, in essence, predates the internet. Businesses have long used referral programs as a way to expand their reach by incentivizing customers to spread the word about their products or services. However, it was with the advent of the internet that affiliate marketing truly came into its own.

The Dawn of Online Affiliate Marketing:

Affiliate marketing as we know it today started in the mid-1990s. The pioneering figure is widely considered to be William J. Tobin, the founder of PC Flowers & Gifts. In 1989, Tobin launched a beta version of the Prodigy Network, which became one of the earliest online affiliate programs. Tobin patented his idea in 2000, officially recognized as the progenitor of the model.

Amazon's Influence: However, it was online retail giant Amazon that truly brought affiliate marketing to the mainstream in 1996 with the launch of its "Associates Program." This program allowed website owners to link to Amazon products and earn a commission on any purchases made through these links. Given Amazon's wide range of products and its burgeoning popularity, this opened up a vast number of opportunities for affiliates.

Growth and Maturation: Since those early days, affiliate marketing has seen steady growth and evolution.

The late 1990s and early 2000s saw a proliferation of affiliate networks like Commission Junction and ClickBank, which served as intermediaries between merchants and affiliates. These networks made it easier for affiliates to find suitable programs and for merchants to manage their affiliate relationships.

In the mid to late 2000s, the growth of social media platforms and blogging provided new avenues for affiliate marketing. Influencers on platforms like Instagram, YouTube, and Facebook, as well as bloggers, started leveraging their followers and readers as potential customers for their affiliate marketing endeavors.

Current Trends: Today, affiliate marketing is a multi-billion dollar industry. It has adapted to changes in technology and consumer behavior, incorporating strategies like SEO

(Search Engine Optimization), email marketing, content marketing, and more.

New trends such as mobile marketing, AI (Artificial Intelligence), and data analytics continue to shape the industry.

As we move further into the 21st century, affiliate marketing remains a viable and attractive online business model due to its cost-effectiveness, scalability, and potential for passive income. However, like any business, it requires knowledge, effort, and strategic planning to succeed, which is what this book aims to provide.

1.3 IMPORTANCE OF AFFILIATE MARKETING IN TODAY'S DIGITAL WORLD

In today's increasingly digital-centric world, affiliate marketing has assumed a pivotal role in the business strategies of many companies, while also providing individuals and smaller entities an opportunity to generate income.

Here are several reasons why affiliate marketing is particularly important in the current digital landscape:

1. **Broadening Customer Reach:** In the vast expanse of the internet, affiliate marketing serves as a bridge that connects products and services with potential customers who might otherwise remain oblivious to them.

Affiliates, with their diverse and wide-ranging platforms, can introduce these offerings to new audiences, thus extending the merchant's reach.

2. **Cost-effectiveness:** For businesses, one of the most appealing aspects of affiliate marketing is its cost-effectiveness. Since payment is made only when a desired action (click, lead, or sale) is accomplished, companies can avoid the significant upfront costs associated with traditional advertising. This pay-for-performance model reduces financial risk and ensures that marketing budgets are spent efficiently.

3. Trust and Credibility: Affiliate marketers often have established relationships with their audience, built on trust and credibility. Recommendations from these trusted sources can significantly influence purchasing decisions. In an era where consumers are often skeptical of traditional advertising, this word-of-mouth marketing can prove highly effective.

4. Data-Driven Marketing: The digital nature of affiliate marketing allows for precise tracking, measurement, and attribution of marketing activities. Merchants can gain valuable insights into customer behavior, preferences, and trends. This data-driven approach enables optimization of marketing strategies, leading to better ROI (Return on Investment).

5. Passive Income Generation: For individuals and influencers, affiliate marketing presents an opportunity to earn passive income. Once the affiliate content (like a blog post or a social media update) featuring the affiliate link is out in the digital space, it can continue to generate revenue without requiring constant effort.

6. Scalability: As businesses grow, their affiliate programs can scale alongside them without the need for significant additional resources. Similarly, successful affiliate marketers can increase their earnings by promoting more products or leveraging more platforms.

7. Adaptability to Market Changes: The current digital market is highly dynamic, with new products, services, and trends emerging constantly. Affiliate marketing offers the flexibility to adapt to these changes, with affiliates being able to switch their focus depending on what's popular or in-demand at any given time.

As we delve further into the topic in subsequent chapters, we will see how these advantages can be effectively harnessed to maximize the potential of affiliate marketing.

Affiliate marketing presents a compelling opportunity for both businesses and individuals, but it also comes with its own set of challenges. Let's delve into both the advantages and disadvantages of this marketing model:

Advantages of Affiliate Marketing:

1. <u>Performance-Based Payments:</u> Businesses only pay when desired actions (click, sale, or lead) are achieved, reducing marketing costs and financial risks.

2. <u>Broad Audience Reach:</u> With affiliates leveraging diverse platforms and catering to different niches, businesses can reach new customers they might otherwise miss.

3. <u>Minimal Start-up Costs:</u> For individuals, affiliate marketing can be started with minimal investment. All that's required is a digital platform (like a blog or social media account) and time to create content.

---

4. Passive Income: Once affiliate content is created and published, it can continue generating income even when the affiliate is not actively working.

5. Flexibility: Affiliates have the freedom to choose the products or services they want to promote, and they can work from anywhere at any time.

6. Scalability: Both merchants and affiliates can easily scale their efforts. Merchants can recruit more affiliates, while affiliates can promote more products or use more platforms.

Disadvantages of Affiliate Marketing:

1. Dependence on Affiliates: Businesses are reliant on affiliates to drive traffic and conversions, which can be unpredictable and inconsistent.

2. Quality Control: It can be challenging for businesses to control how their products or services are represented by affiliates, which could potentially harm their brand.

3. Competition: The affiliate marketing space is highly competitive. Affiliates often compete against each other for audience attention, while businesses vie for the most effective affiliates.

4. Fraud: Like many online industries, affiliate marketing is susceptible to fraudulent activities, such as click fraud or cookie stuffing. This can lead to skewed data and unjust payouts.

5. Time and Effort: Successful affiliate marketing requires significant time and effort. Building a platform, generating traffic, and creating quality content that drives conversions is not an overnight process.

6. Payment Issues: Affiliates sometimes face issues with payment delays, low commission rates, or stringent payout thresholds.

By understanding these potential benefits and challenges, you can make informed decisions and strategies to maximize the advantages and mitigate the disadvantages as you embark on your affiliate marketing journey.

2.1 THE KEY PLAYERS: MERCHANTS, NETWORKS, PUBLISHERS, AND CUSTOMERS

Understanding the dynamics of the affiliate marketing ecosystem requires a grasp of the roles and responsibilities of its key players.

Here's a breakdown of who they are and what they do:

1. Merchants: Merchants, also known as advertisers or retailers, are businesses that sell a product or service. They create the affiliate programs to incentivize other parties to promote their offerings. Merchants could range from small businesses to multinational corporations, and they can operate in various industries such as fashion, technology, travel, and more. In the context of affiliate marketing, they handle the product creation, order fulfillment, and customer service.

2. Affiliate Networks: Affiliate networks act as intermediaries between merchants and publishers. They provide a platform where merchants can list their affiliate programs, and publishers can find programs that align with their niche.

The network tracks clicks, conversions, and commissions and generally handles the administrative tasks like payment processing. Examples of popular affiliate networks include ClickBank, Commission Junction (CJ), and Amazon Associates. However, it's worth noting that not all affiliate programs operate through a network; some merchants run their programs in-house.

3. Publishers/Affiliates: Publishers, also referred to as affiliates or marketers, are individuals or companies that promote the merchant's products or services. They do this by placing affiliate links on their digital platforms, such as blogs, websites, social media accounts, or email newsletters. When their audience members click on these links and perform the desired action (like making a purchase), the publishers earn a commission.

Successful affiliates typically have a strong online presence and a dedicated audience that trusts their recommendations.

4. Customers: Customers are the consumers who click on the affiliate links and perform the desired action, such as making a purchase, signing up for a service, or filling out a form. They are the driving force behind affiliate marketing. The transaction is usually seamless for the customer, and it doesn't cost them extra to purchase through an affiliate link. In fact, sometimes they may benefit from exclusive deals or discounts offered by the affiliate. Each of these players is crucial to the successful functioning of the affiliate marketing system. As we explore further, we'll look into the specific roles and strategies for succeeding as an affiliate.

Affiliate networks play a crucial role in the affiliate marketing landscape, serving as a bridge between merchants and affiliates. They essentially streamline the process for both parties, making it easier and more efficient.

Here are the main roles and responsibilities of affiliate networks:

1. Program Management: Affiliate networks manage the affiliate programs on behalf of merchants. This involves everything from tracking sales, clicks, and leads to processing payments and handling disputes. By taking care of these administrative tasks, they allow merchants to focus more on their product or service.

2. Affiliate Recruitment and Support: Networks are actively involved in recruiting affiliates for the programs they host. They offer support to these affiliates, providing them with the necessary links, banners, and other promotional materials.

Additionally, they handle affiliate inquiries and provide training or guidance as needed.

3. Tracking and Reporting: One of the key roles of an affiliate network is to provide accurate tracking of affiliate activities and comprehensive reporting. Networks use sophisticated tracking software to monitor the performance of each affiliate. This allows merchants to see which affiliates are driving sales and affiliates to see their earnings and performance metrics.

4. Payment Processing: Affiliate networks handle the payment process. They calculate the commissions earned by each affiliate and process payments based on the terms of the affiliate program. This relieves merchants of the administrative burden of processing numerous payments.

5. Quality Assurance and Compliance: Affiliate networks also ensure that both merchants and affiliates adhere to the agreed terms and conditions. They work to maintain a high standard of quality and compliance, which helps to build trust and credibility in the affiliate marketing industry.

In short, affiliate networks facilitate the relationship between merchants and affiliates, ensuring that everything runs smoothly. They provide a centralized platform where merchants can efficiently manage their affiliate programs, and affiliates can find and participate in programs that align with their niche. However, it's important for both parties to conduct thorough research and due diligence when choosing an affiliate network, as the quality and service can vary between networks.

2.3 THE AFFILIATE MARKETING VALUE CHAIN

The affiliate marketing value chain is a step-by-step process that traces the flow of value from the initial product or service to the final consumer, through the various stakeholders in the affiliate marketing ecosystem. It's a sequence of activities that create and build value at each step.

Here's how it works:

1. Product/Service Creation: The process starts with the merchant, who creates a product or a service. The merchant decides to use affiliate marketing as a strategy to promote their offering and, therefore, sets up an affiliate program, either independently or through an affiliate network.

2. Affiliate Program Management: The affiliate program management could be handled by the merchant or, as is often the case, by an affiliate network. The network or the merchant's in-house program manager is responsible for tracking sales or leads generated by affiliates, calculating commissions, and making payments.

3. Publisher/Affiliate Recruitment: Affiliates or publishers are recruited to join the affiliate program. They are selected based on factors like their platform relevance, audience size, audience engagement, etc. Once recruited, they receive access to the promotional materials like banners, text links, or unique affiliate codes.

4. Promotion of Products/Services: Affiliates promote the merchant's products or services on their platforms, which could be blogs, social media accounts, email newsletters, etc. This is usually done through content marketing strategies - creating engaging and valuable content that naturally incorporates the affiliate links.

5. Customer Action: A potential customer, who is a part of the affiliate's audience, clicks on the affiliate link and is directed to the merchant's website. If the customer takes the desired action (such as making a purchase or signing up for a service), the affiliate earns a commission.

6. Sales and Revenue: The merchant gains a sale, the affiliate earns a commission, and the customer receives the product or service they desired. This cycle continues, creating a sustainable model of revenue generation.

Understanding this value chain can help you visualize the interconnectedness of the different components of affiliate marketing and how value is created and transferred at each stage. As we move further, we'll dive deeper into each of these stages, discussing strategies and best practices to maximize the effectiveness of your affiliate marketing efforts.

2.4 THE LIFE CYCLE OF AN AFFILIATE MARKETING CAMPAIGN

The life cycle of an affiliate marketing campaign can be broken down into several stages. Each stage requires careful planning and execution to ensure the success of the campaign.

Let's take a look at these stages:

1. **Planning and Research:** Before starting any campaign, it's crucial to conduct thorough research and planning. This involves understanding your audience, identifying suitable affiliate programs, selecting products or services that align with your niche, and defining your marketing goals. It also involves keyword research for SEO purposes and content planning.

2. Joining an Affiliate Program: Once you've identified a suitable affiliate program, the next step is to join it. This usually involves filling out an application form and waiting for approval. Some programs accept affiliates instantly, while others review applications before accepting them.

3. Campaign Creation: After joining an affiliate program, you'll need to create your marketing campaign. This involves producing engaging content that incorporates your affiliate links, such as blog posts, reviews, social media posts, or email newsletters. The goal is to provide valuable content to your audience while subtly encouraging them to click on your affiliate links.

4. Promotion and Marketing: Once your content is ready, the next stage is promotion and marketing. This could involve SEO tactics to improve your search engine rankings, social media marketing, email marketing, or even paid advertising. The aim is to drive as much traffic as possible to your content and thereby to your affiliate links.

5. Conversion and Sales: If your marketing efforts are successful, your audience will click on your affiliate links and be directed to the merchant's website. If they then make a purchase or carry out the desired action, you earn a commission.

6. Review and Optimization: The final stage of the cycle involves reviewing the performance of your campaign and optimizing for better results. Most affiliate programs provide performance metrics, such as click-through rates (CTR), conversion rates, and revenue. Analyzing these metrics can provide valuable insights into what's working and what's not, allowing you to make data-driven decisions to improve your campaign. Remember, affiliate marketing is not a set-and-forget strategy. It requires continuous effort, testing, and optimization to succeed.

The life cycle repeats as you learn from your experiences, adjust your strategies, and launch new campaigns. This continuous learning and adaptation is what makes affiliate marketing both a challenge and an exciting opportunity.

3.1 OVERVIEW OF INTERNET MARKETING

Internet marketing, also known as online marketing or digital marketing, refers to the strategies used to market products or services over the internet. It's a broad field that encompasses a variety of tactics, tools, and platforms, all aimed at reaching a global audience, building brand awareness, and driving conversions.

Here's an overview of the main components:

1. Website Marketing: A company's website often serves as the hub of its internet marketing efforts. Websites are used to showcase products or services, provide information, and facilitate sales. They also play a crucial role in other internet marketing strategies, such as content marketing, SEO, and email marketing.

2. Search Engine Optimization (SEO): SEO involves optimizing a website and its content to achieve higher rankings in search engine results pages (SERPs). This increases the website's visibility, drives organic (non-paid) traffic, and enhances user experience.

3. Content Marketing: This strategy involves creating and sharing valuable free content to attract and convert prospects into customers, and customers into repeat buyers. The type of content you share is closely related to what you sell. Blogs, videos, podcasts, infographics, and social media posts are all examples of content marketing materials.

4. Social Media Marketing: This involves promoting your brand, products, or services on social media platforms like Facebook, Instagram, Twitter, LinkedIn, and others. It's not just about posting ads; it's also about engaging with your audience, building a community, and enhancing your brand's presence.

5. Email Marketing: Email marketing is a direct marketing strategy that uses email to promote products or services, nurture relationships with prospects or customers, and encourage repeat business. This might involve sending out newsletters, promotional offers, or personalized recommendations.

6. Pay-Per-Click (PPC) Advertising: In PPC advertising, advertisers pay a fee each time one of their ads is clicked. It's essentially a way of buying visits to your site, rather than attempting to earn them organically. Google Ads is one of the most popular PPC advertising platforms.

7. Affiliate Marketing: As we've been discussing, affiliate marketing involves promoting other companies' products or services in exchange for a commission on any sales or leads that result from your promotion. Internet marketing is a dynamic and multi-faceted field, offering businesses of all sizes the opportunity to reach a wider audience and drive sales in a cost-effective way. Understanding how these components interrelate and support each other is key to creating an effective internet marketing strategy.

Search Engine Optimization (SEO) is a fundamental component of successful affiliate marketing. It's the process of improving your website's visibility in organic search engine results to attract more traffic. Here, we'll explore the basics of SEO and why it's so important in affiliate marketing.

Basics of SEO:

1. Keyword Research: This involves finding and analyzing the terms that people enter into search engines. The aim is to use this information to create content around these keywords.

2. On-Page SEO: This includes all the measures that can be taken within your website to improve its position in search rankings. This involves optimizing elements like title tags, meta descriptions, URLs, and content.

3. Off-Page SEO: This involves activities that occur outside your website but affect your site's search engine rankings. It primarily refers to backlinks from other websites, but also includes social signals and other marketing activities outside your own website.

4. Technical SEO: This refers to the process of optimizing your website for crawling and indexing by search engines, but can also include any other technical means to improve search visibility, such as enhancing site speed, mobile-friendliness, and website architecture.

Importance of SEO in Affiliate Marketing:

1. Driving Traffic: The higher your website ranks in search engine results, the more visibility you have, and the more likely users are to visit your site. This is essential for affiliates as it can directly lead to higher click-through rates on affiliate links and, consequently, more conversions.

2. Cost-Effective: Unlike paid advertising, organic traffic from SEO is "free." Investing in SEO can provide a sustainable and cost-effective source of traffic over the long term.

3. Trust and Credibility: Users generally perceive the top results in search engines as more trustworthy and credible. As an affiliate, appearing high in search results can enhance your reputation and improve click-through rates.

4. Better User Experience: Good SEO involves optimizing not just for search engines but also for users. This means creating high-quality, relevant content, ensuring your site is fast and mobile-friendly, and providing a good user experience, all of which can also improve your chances of successful affiliate marketing.

In the context of affiliate marketing, understanding and leveraging SEO is essential. It's a valuable tool for driving organic traffic to your site, enhancing your online presence, and ultimately boosting your affiliate earnings.

Pay-Per-Click (PPC) advertising is a model of internet marketing in which advertisers pay a fee each time one of their ads is clicked. Essentially, it's a way of buying visits to your site, rather than attempting to earn those visits organically through SEO. Here's a basic breakdown of how it works:

1. Setting Up a PPC Campaign: To run a PPC campaign, you'll need to set up an account on a PPC platform. The most popular platform is Google Ads, but there are others such as Bing Ads or Facebook Ads. Once you've set up an account, you can create your ads, choose your target audience, set your budget, and decide on the keywords you want to target.

2. How PPC Ads Work: When a user performs a search using one of your chosen keywords, your ad has the potential to appear in the search results, typically at the top or bottom of the page. This placement is determined by an auction-style process in which you and other advertisers bid on your chosen keywords. If your bid is among the highest, your ad will be displayed.

3. Paying for Clicks: As the name suggests, with PPC, you only pay when someone actually clicks on your ad. The cost of each click (CPC) can vary depending on the keyword and the competition for that keyword. You can set a maximum CPC to ensure you don't spend more than you're comfortable with.

4. Tracking and Optimizing: Most PPC platforms provide tools for tracking the performance of your ads. You can see how many people have seen your ad (impressions), how many clicked on it (clicks), and how many took the desired action after clicking (conversions). You can use this data to optimize your ads and improve your return on investment.

5. Importance in Affiliate Marketing: For affiliate marketers, PPC can be a valuable tool for driving traffic to your site or directly to the merchant's site through your affiliate link. It can be especially useful when you're just starting out and don't have a large organic reach yet. However, it's important to keep in mind that you'll be paying for each click, so you need to carefully manage your budget and ensure that the cost of your PPC campaign doesn't exceed the revenue it generates.

3.4 THE ROLE OF CONTENT MARKETING

Content marketing is a strategic approach focused on creating and distributing valuable, relevant, and consistent content to attract and retain a clearly-defined audience, and ultimately, to drive profitable customer action.

Let's look at how it plays out and why it's vital in affiliate marketing:

Understanding Content Marketing:

Content marketing is about storytelling and providing useful information to consumers, rather than directly selling a product or service. The content you create should be relevant to your audience and offer value, such as solving a problem they have, answering a question, or offering advice.

There are various forms of content marketing, including blog posts, videos, podcasts, infographics, webinars, social media content, and more. The type of content you create will depend on your audience and what they are most likely to engage with.

Role of Content Marketing in Affiliate Marketing:

1. Building Trust: By producing high-quality content that's valuable to your audience, you build a relationship with them, which in turn fosters trust. When you recommend a product or service through affiliate marketing, that trust can lead to higher click-through and conversion rates.

2. Driving Traffic: Content marketing, especially when combined with SEO, can significantly increase traffic to your website. The more people that visit your site, the higher the chances of them clicking on your affiliate links.

3. Enhancing SEO: Search engines reward websites that publish quality, consistent content. As your content improves and attracts more traffic, your site will rise in the search

rankings, leading to more visibility and more potential for clicks on your affiliate links.

4. Encouraging Conversions: Content marketing allows you to subtly promote products or services within the valuable content you're providing. A well-placed affiliate link in a compelling blog post or video can lead to high conversion rates.

5. Establishing Authority: Creating informative, useful content can establish you as an authority in your field. This perceived expertise can make your audience more likely to trust your recommendations and click on your affiliate links.

In the realm of affiliate marketing, content is the vehicle that carries your affiliate links to your audience. Without valuable content, it's difficult to attract and retain the audience necessary to generate affiliate revenue. Thus, a solid content marketing strategy is indispensable for successful affiliate marketing.

4.1 UNDERSTANDING YOUR PLATFORM OPTIONS

As an affiliate marketer, the platform you choose to use plays a critical role in your ability to successfully connect with your audience and promote affiliate products or services. Below, we'll discuss some of the most popular platform options available:

1. **Websites/Blogs:** Having your own website or blog gives you a lot of control over your affiliate marketing. You can easily incorporate affiliate links into your content, whether that's in blog posts, product reviews, or resource pages. Plus, by optimizing your website for SEO, you can attract organic traffic from search engines.

2. **Social Media:** Platforms like Facebook, Instagram, Twitter, and Pinterest can be used to promote affiliate products. By building a following on social media, you can promote products to your followers by incorporating affiliate links into

your posts, stories, or bio. Keep in mind that each platform has different rules about affiliate links, so be sure to understand these.

3. YouTube: Creating video content for YouTube is another way to engage in affiliate marketing. You can create product reviews, tutorials, or other types of content related to the affiliate products you're promoting, and include your affiliate links in the video description.

4. Podcasts: Podcasting has exploded in popularity in recent years, and it presents another opportunity for affiliate marketing. You can promote products in your podcast episodes and include your affiliate links in the episode descriptions or show notes.

5. Email Newsletters: Building an email list and sending out regular newsletters can be an effective way to promote affiliate products. You can include affiliate links in your newsletters when you talk about relevant products or services.

Each platform has its pros and cons, and the right choice depends on a variety of factors, including your target audience, your preferred format (text, audio, video), and where your skills lie. In many cases, using a combination of platforms can be the most effective approach. For instance, you might use a blog for in-depth content and SEO purposes, social media for engagement and brand awareness, and an email newsletter for direct communication with your audience.

4.2 BUILDING YOUR OWN WEBSITE: TIPS AND STRATEGIES

Building your own website is often the first step in starting an affiliate marketing business. A website serves as a hub where you can create and share content, engage with your audience, and promote affiliate products. Here are some tips and strategies to help you get started:

1. Choose a Suitable Platform: There are numerous website building platforms available today, including WordPress, Wix, and Squarespace, among others. WordPress is often the preferred choice for affiliate marketers due to its flexibility, SEO

capabilities, and the availability of various plugins to facilitate affiliate marketing.

2. Choose a Domain and Hosting Provider: Select a domain name that is relevant to your niche and easy for users to remember. Also, choose a reliable hosting provider. Some popular options include Bluehost, SiteGround, and HostGator.

3. Design a User-Friendly Website: Ensure your website is easy to navigate with a clean, attractive design. A well-structured website enhances user experience and can improve SEO. Remember, your goal is to guide visitors to your affiliate links in a natural, intuitive way.

4. Create Quality Content: The content on your website is key to attracting visitors and converting them into customers. Create valuable, informative content related to your niche and incorporate your affiliate links in a way that adds value for your readers.

5. Optimize for SEO: Optimize your website and content for search engines to increase your visibility. This includes using relevant keywords, creating quality backlinks, ensuring your site is mobile-friendly, and improving page load speeds.

6. Build an Email List: Include an email sign-up form on your website to start building an email list. This gives you a direct line of communication with your audience and can be a powerful tool for promoting affiliate products.

7. Monitor and Optimize: Use tools like Google Analytics to monitor your website's performance. Analyze metrics like page views, bounce rate, and conversion rate to understand what's working and what needs improvement.

Building your own website can be a big task, but with these tips, you'll be well on your way to creating a platform that can support a successful affiliate marketing business.

Social media platforms can be effective tools for affiliate marketers, allowing them to reach a broad audience and engage with them in a more personal way. Here's how you can leverage social media for your affiliate marketing efforts:

1. Choose the Right Platforms: Different social media platforms attract different audiences. Instagram and Pinterest are ideal for visually appealing products, while Twitter might be better for quick updates and direct interaction. LinkedIn can be useful for B2B products, and Facebook offers a mix of formats. Choose the platforms that align with your target audience and product niche.

2. Create Engaging Content: Like any marketing strategy, success on social media comes from providing value. Create engaging, high-quality content that aligns with your audience's interests. This could be product reviews, tutorials, or tips related to your niche. Remember to weave in your affiliate products naturally and authentically.

3. Utilize Each Platform's Unique Features: Take advantage of each platform's unique features. For instance, use Instagram Stories or Facebook Live for behind-the-scenes content, demonstrations, or Q&A sessions. Utilize Pinterest's boards to categorize your affiliate products.

4. Be Transparent About Affiliate Links: Most social media platforms require users to disclose when a post contains an affiliate link. This could be as simple as using a hashtag like #ad or #affiliate. Always follow each platform's rules regarding this to maintain trust with your audience.

5. Engage with Your Followers: Social media is a two-way street. Respond to comments, answer questions, and engage with other users' content. This helps to build a community around your brand and can increase your reach.

6. Use Social Media Advertising: If your budget allows, consider social media advertising to extend your reach. Most platforms offer highly targeted advertising options, ensuring your content reaches the right people.

7. Track Your Performance: Use analytics to monitor how well your posts are performing. Most social media platforms offer in-built analytics tools that allow you to track engagement, click-through rates, and conversions. Use this data to refine your strategy over time.

Remember, social media success doesn't happen overnight. It requires consistent effort, so be patient and persistent. With time and the right strategy, social media can become a powerful channel for your affiliate marketing business.

Email marketing can be an incredibly effective tool in an affiliate marketer's arsenal, offering direct access to potential customers. Here are some strategies for leveraging email marketing as an affiliate tool:

1. **Build Your Subscriber List:** The first step in email marketing is to build a subscriber list. You can do this by offering a newsletter subscription on your website or blog, providing a free downloadable resource in exchange for an email address, or promoting your email list on social media platforms.

2. **Deliver Value:** Before promoting any affiliate products, it's important to establish trust and rapport with your audience. You can achieve this by consistently delivering valuable content. This might include industry news, tips and tricks, educational resources, or exclusive content that they can't find on your other platforms.

3. Personalize Your Emails: Many email marketing platforms allow you to personalize emails, which can increase open rates and engagement. Personalization can be as simple as addressing the recipient by their first name, or more advanced techniques like segmenting your list and sending tailored content based on subscribers' interests or behaviors.

4. Incorporate Affiliate Links Naturally: Your affiliate promotions should feel like a natural part of your email content. This could be a product you're discussing in a tutorial, a tool you're recommending, or a relevant product offer at the end of an informative email.

5. Use a Strong Call to Action: Every email you send should have a clear and compelling call to action (CTA). This might be 'click here to learn more', 'buy now', or 'download your free guide'. Your CTA should lead the reader to click on your affiliate link.

6. Monitor and Optimize: Use your email marketing platform's analytics to monitor open rates, click-through rates, and conversions. Look for patterns and trends to understand what types of content and promotions are most effective, and use this information to optimize your future emails.

7. Maintain Compliance: It's essential to follow laws and regulations related to email marketing, such as the CAN-SPAM Act in the United States or GDPR in Europe. This includes getting consent from subscribers before sending them emails, providing a clear way for them to opt out, and disclosing when you're using affiliate links.

By building a strong relationship with your email subscribers and delivering consistent value, you can create a highly effective channel for promoting your affiliate products.

5.1 THE IMPORTANCE OF CHOOSING A NICHE

Choosing a niche is a critical first step in establishing a successful affiliate marketing business. A niche is a specialized segment of the market that you'll focus your efforts on.

Here's why it's so important:

1. **Targeted Audience:** When you choose a specific niche, you can target a more defined audience. This audience will likely be more engaged, as your content and the products you promote are more directly aligned with their interests and needs.

2. **Less Competition:** Broad markets can be highly competitive, making it hard for newcomers to stand out. In contrast, a narrower niche will often have less competition, making it easier for you to establish a presence and build a reputation.

3. Greater Expertise: Focusing on a niche allows you to build deep expertise in that area. This expertise can make your content more valuable and credible, which can enhance trust with your audience and make them more likely to click on your affiliate links.

4. Easier Content Creation: When you're deeply familiar with a specific niche, it can be easier to come up with content ideas and to write or create that content. This can make your affiliate marketing efforts more sustainable in the long term.

5. Better Relationships with Merchants: If you're known for your focus and expertise in a particular niche, you may find it easier to establish relationships with merchants in that niche. They'll see you as a valuable partner who can reach a highly targeted audience.

Choosing a niche isn't about limiting your options; it's about focusing your efforts in a way that will yield the best results. By selecting a niche that aligns with your interests and expertise, you can create a strong foundation for your affiliate marketing business.

Once you understand the importance of choosing a niche for your affiliate marketing business, the next step is to identify potential niches that could be profitable.

Here are some strategies to guide your research:

1. **Identify Your Interests and Passions:** Successful affiliate marketing often involves creating a lot of content around your chosen niche, so it helps if it's a topic you're passionate about. Start by listing your hobbies, interests, or areas of expertise.

2. **Research Market Demand:** Use tools like Google Trends, Keyword Planner, and SEMRush to assess the demand for different niches. Look for niches that have consistent interest over time and that people are actively searching for.

3. Assess the Competition: You want a niche that isn't overly saturated, but it's also important to ensure there's at least some competition - this indicates that the niche is profitable. Tools like SEMRush or Ahrefs can help you analyze your competition.

4. Identify Potential Affiliate Programs: Look for niches that have a variety of affiliate programs and products. Websites like ClickBank, ShareASale, and Amazon Associates can give you an idea of the types of products available in different niches.

5. Consider Profit Potential: Some niches may have a high volume of interest, but low-priced products. Other niches may have higher-priced products, but lower volume. Consider both factors when assessing a niche's profit potential.

6. Evaluate Long-Term Potential: Finally, consider the long-term potential of the niche. Trends can offer short-term profit opportunities, but for long-term success, it's best to choose a niche with enduring appeal.

Identifying a profitable niche is a balance between finding a topic you're passionate about, and ensuring there's enough market demand and profit potential. This research process can take time, but it's a crucial step in setting up a successful affiliate marketing business.

5.3 EVALUATING NICHE COMPETITION

Once you've identified potential niches for your affiliate marketing business, the next step is to evaluate the competition within those niches. Understanding your competition can provide insights into market saturation, identify gaps that you can fill, and help you position your business effectively.

Here's how to go about evaluating niche competition:

1. **Conduct a Google Search:** Start with a simple Google search for keywords associated with your potential niche.

If the first page of results is dominated by large, established brands, it could be a sign that the niche is highly competitive.

2. Analyze Keyword Difficulty: Use SEO tools like SEMRush, Ahrefs, or Moz to analyze keyword difficulty. This will give you an idea of how hard it will be to rank on search engines for your niche-related keywords. A high keyword difficulty often indicates high competition.

3. Review Affiliate Networks: Check affiliate networks like ClickBank, ShareASale, or Amazon Associates to see how many products are available in your potential niche and how many affiliates are promoting them. A high number of products with a high number of affiliates could indicate a competitive niche.

4. Use Social Media: Look at the presence of your potential niche on social media. If there are many pages or accounts with a large following dedicated to this niche, it could suggest high competition.

5. Check Out Online Forums and Communities: Sites like Quora, Reddit, or niche-specific forums can give you an

idea of how many people are actively involved in a community related to your potential niche.

6. Analyze the Quality of Existing Content: Look at the quality of the content your competitors are producing. If it's high-quality, it means you'll need to match or exceed that level to compete. If it's lower quality, it could be an opportunity for you to stand out with superior content.

Remember, while high competition can make it harder for you to stand out, it also indicates that a niche is profitable. On the other hand, a niche with little competition may be less profitable, but it could also offer the opportunity to become a leading authority. The key is to find a balance that suits your goals and capabilities.

After researching potential niches, identifying profitable ones, and evaluating competition, it's time to commit to your chosen niche and start developing it.

Here's how to do it:

1. Make the Commitment: Choosing a niche is a critical decision that will guide your affiliate marketing business. Once you've made your choice, commit to it fully.

Remember that success won't come overnight, and it's important to be patient and persistent.

2. Understand Your Audience: To effectively serve your niche, you must deeply understand your target audience. Learn about their interests, needs, and pain points. What problems can you solve for them? What kinds of content do they find valuable?

3. Choose Relevant Affiliate Programs: Join affiliate programs that offer products or services relevant to your niche.

The more relevant the offerings, the more likely your audience is to engage with your affiliate links.

4. Create High-Quality Content: Consistently create and publish high-quality content that's relevant to your niche and provides value to your audience. This could be blog posts, videos, social media posts, podcasts, or other types of content. Incorporate your affiliate links naturally within this content.

5. Engage with Your Audience: Engage with your audience through comments, emails, social media, and other channels. This can help you build a relationship with them, understand their needs better, and gain their trust.

6. Continuously Learn and Adapt: Stay up-to-date with trends and changes in your niche. Always be learning and be ready to adapt your strategies as necessary.

7. Track Your Progress and Optimize: Use analytics tools to track your progress. Monitor metrics like website traffic,

click-through rates on your affiliate links, and conversion rates. Use this information to understand what's working, what's not, and how you can optimize your strategies.

Remember, developing your niche is not a one-time activity, but an ongoing process. The more time and effort you put into understanding your niche and serving your audience, the more successful your affiliate marketing business can be.

6.1 CRITERIA FOR CHOOSING AFFILIATE PROGRAMS

Choosing the right affiliate programs is crucial to your success as an affiliate marketer.

Here are some key criteria to consider:

1. Relevance: The affiliate program's products or services should be relevant to your niche and your audience. Irrelevant products won't appeal to your audience and can damage your credibility.

2. Quality of Products or Services: The products or services you promote need to be of high quality. Promoting low-quality products can damage your reputation and result in low conversion rates and high return rates.

3. Commission Structure: Look at the program's commission structure. This might include the commission rate, whether it offers one-time or recurring commissions, and how often it pays out. A higher commission rate isn't always better if the product has a low conversion rate.

4. Affiliate Support: Good affiliate programs offer support to their affiliates, such as promotional materials, affiliate training, and dedicated affiliate managers. This can be particularly valuable if you're a beginner.

5. Payment Terms: Consider the program's payment terms. How often do they pay out? Do they offer different payment methods? Is there a minimum payout threshold?

6. Reputation: Check the program's reputation. Look for reviews or ask other affiliates about their experiences. A program with a poor reputation should be a red flag.

7. Cookie Duration: The cookie duration refers to the period during which you can earn a commission after a user clicks your affiliate link. Longer cookie durations are generally better.

8. Conversion Rate: A high-converting product or service can be more profitable than a higher commission rate on a low-converting product. Many affiliate programs will provide information about their conversion rates. Remember, the best affiliate program is the one that aligns with your audience and your business goals. It's often a good idea to test different programs to see which works best for you.

6.2 UNDERSTANDING COMMISSION STRUCTURES

Affiliate programs can have different commission structures, and understanding these can help you choose the most profitable programs to join.

Here are some common types of commission structures:

1. Percentage of Sale: This is the most common type of commission structure in affiliate marketing. You earn a percentage of the sale price each time a customer makes a purchase through your affiliate link. The percentage can vary widely depending on the program and the product.

2. Fixed Amount per Sale: In this case, you earn a fixed amount for each sale, regardless of the sale price. This is common in certain industries, such as financial services.

3. Cost Per Action (CPA): With CPA, you earn a commission when a user performs a specific action, such as signing up for a trial, filling out a form, or making a purchase.

4. Recurring Commissions: Some programs offer recurring commissions for subscription-based products or services. You earn a commission not just on the initial sale, but on all subsequent renewals or recurring charges.

5. Two-Tier Commissions: In a two-tier commission structure, you earn a commission on your direct sales, and also a smaller commission on sales made by affiliates who you referred to the program.

6. Pay Per Click (PPC): This is less common in affiliate marketing, but some programs pay a small commission each time a user clicks on your affiliate link, regardless of whether they make a purchase.

When considering the commission structure, also take into account the product price, the conversion rate, the cookie duration, and the payout terms. A high commission rate can be attractive, but it's not much use if the product is unlikely to convert, or if the payout terms are unfavourable. Always consider the overall potential for earnings when choosing an affiliate program.

6.3 REVIEWING THE PRODUCT OR SERVICE

Before you decide to promote a product or service as an affiliate, it's crucial to review it thoroughly. Your reputation is on the line, and promoting a poor-quality product can harm your credibility with your audience.

Here are some steps you can follow:

1. Use the Product/Service Yourself: The best way to review a product or service is to use it yourself. This allows you to understand its features, benefits, and any potential drawbacks from a user's perspective. If the cost to purchase is prohibitive, you may contact the merchant directly to ask for a free trial or review copy.

2. Research User Reviews: Search online for reviews from other users. Look for reviews on different platforms, including the product's website, online stores, forums, and social media. This can provide a broader perspective on the product's quality, performance, and customer satisfaction.

3. Consider the Product's Reputation: Is the product or service well-known and respected in your niche? Does it come from a reputable company? A product with a good reputation can be easier to promote and may convert better.

4. Evaluate the Sales Page: Visit the product's sales page and evaluate it from a customer's perspective. Is it appealing and persuasive? Does it provide all the necessary information? If the sales page is poorly designed or lacks key information, it may be harder to convert your traffic into sales.

5. Check for Customer Support: A product or service with strong customer support can lead to higher satisfaction among your audience members if they decide to purchase. Check what kind of support the merchant provides, such as live chat, email, or a knowledge base.

Remember, as an affiliate, you're recommending products to your audience. It's important to ensure that what you're promoting is of high quality and valuable to your audience. By thoroughly reviewing the product, you can ensure you're providing the best recommendations, which can lead to higher trust, better conversion rates, and more affiliate revenue.

6.4 CONSIDERING AFFILIATE PROGRAM SUPPORT AND RESOURCES

Support and resources provided by an affiliate program are crucial factors to consider, especially for beginners. They can significantly aid in your marketing efforts and increase your chances of success. Here's what to look for:

1. Dedicated Affiliate Manager: Some programs provide a dedicated affiliate manager who can answer your questions, provide insights, and assist you in maximizing your earnings. A responsive and knowledgeable manager can be a great asset.

2. Promotional Materials: Many affiliate programs offer a variety of promotional materials you can use, including banners, product images, email swipes, and even pre-written content. These can save you time and make it easier to promote their products.

3. Training and Education: Check if the program provides any training or educational resources. These could be tutorials, webinars, guides, or case studies that can help you understand their products better and learn effective promotional strategies.

4. Reporting Tools: A good affiliate program will provide a dashboard or reporting tool where you can track your clicks, conversions, and earnings. This data is crucial for understanding what's working and what's not, and for optimizing your strategies.

5. Active Affiliate Community: Some programs have an active community of affiliates, often in the form of a private forum or Facebook group. This can be a great place to learn from other affiliates, get ideas, and stay up-to-date with the program.

6. Reliable and Transparent Payout System: Make sure the program has a reliable system for tracking sales and paying commissions. You should be able to trust that you'll be paid accurately and on time.

Remember, the more support and resources an affiliate program offers, the easier it will be for you to promote their products effectively. While these factors shouldn't be the only thing you consider when choosing a program, they can definitely make your affiliate marketing journey smoother and more profitable.

7.1 THE IMPORTANCE OF TRANSPARENCY AND HONESTY

Building trust and credibility with your audience is critical in affiliate marketing. This is where transparency and honesty come into play.

Here are some reasons why they are important:

1. **Builds Trust with Your Audience:** Being open and honest about your affiliations and the products you're promoting helps your audience trust you. If they believe that you're recommending a product simply because you stand to earn a commission, without believing in the product yourself, they're less likely to follow your recommendations.

2. Avoids Audience Alienation: Hiding your affiliations or being dishonest about the products you're promoting can alienate your audience when they discover the truth. This can

lead to a loss of followers, decreased engagement, and lower conversions.

3. Complies with Legal Requirements: In many countries, disclosing your affiliate relationships is a legal requirement. The Federal Trade Commission (FTC) in the U.S., for example, requires that you disclose your affiliate links to your audience.

4. Enhances Your Reputation: Honesty enhances your reputation not just with your audience, but also with other marketers and affiliate programs. This can open up opportunities for partnerships and collaborations.

To maintain transparency and honesty:

- Always disclose your affiliate relationships to your audience. Let them know that you'll earn a commission if they purchase through your link.

- Only promote products you have used, tested, or thoroughly researched.

- Be honest about the pros and cons of the products you promote. No product is perfect, and your audience will appreciate your honesty.

- Don't make exaggerated claims about a product's capabilities or potential benefits.

Remember, your audience is fundamental to your success in affiliate marketing. Maintaining their trust through transparency and honesty is essential.

7.2 BUILDING A PERSONAL BRAND

Building a personal brand can greatly enhance your credibility and trustworthiness in affiliate marketing. A strong personal brand sets you apart from the competition and gives your audience a reason to choose you over others. Here's how you can go about it:

1. Define Your Brand: Start by defining what your personal brand is all about. What's your unique selling proposition?

What values do you stand for? What's your voice and personality? Be clear on these aspects as they form the core of your brand.

2. Showcase Your Expertise: To build credibility, it's important to demonstrate your expertise in your niche. This could be through high-quality blog posts, insightful videos, informative social media updates, speaking engagements, or even publishing a book.

3. Be Consistent: Consistency is key in branding. From your logo and website design to your writing style and the content you share, everything should be consistent and align with your brand. This creates a unified image in the minds of your audience.

4. Engage with Your Audience: Engaging directly with your audience helps build a relationship with them, which is crucial for trust. Respond to comments, answer questions, ask

for feedback, and show appreciation for their support. Show them that there's a real person behind the brand.

5. Be Authentic: Authenticity is highly valued today. Don't try to be someone you're not, just to please your audience. Be true to yourself, and don't be afraid to share your thoughts, opinions, and even your mistakes.

6. Keep Learning and Improving: No matter how much you know, there's always more to learn. Continually investing in your skills and knowledge not only improves your effectiveness as an affiliate marketer, but also demonstrates your commitment to your niche.

7. Monitor Your Online Reputation: Use online tools to monitor mentions of your name or brand. This can help you manage your reputation, respond to negative comments, and understand what your audience thinks of you. Remember, building a personal brand is a long-term endeavor. It won't happen overnight, but with consistency and effort, you can

create a brand that resonates with your audience and enhances your success in affiliate marketing.

Creating valuable and relevant content is at the heart of affiliate marketing. This content not only drives traffic and generates leads, but it also helps you build trust and credibility with your audience. Here are some steps to help you create content that resonates with your audience:

1. Know Your Audience: Before you start creating content, it's essential to have a clear understanding of your audience. What are their needs, interests, and challenges? What type of content do they prefer? Use this information to create content that speaks directly to them.

2. Provide Value: Your content should provide value to your audience. This could be in the form of information, solutions, insights, or entertainment. The more value you provide, the more likely your audience is to trust you and consider your recommendations.

3. Be Relevant: Keep your content relevant to your niche and the products you're promoting. Irrelevant content can confuse your audience and make you lose credibility.

4. Use a Mix of Content Types: Different people prefer different types of content. Use a mix of blog posts, videos, infographics, podcasts, and social media updates to engage your audience. Experiment to find out what works best for your audience.

5. Update Regularly: Regularly updating your content not only keeps your audience engaged, but it also helps with SEO (Search Engine Optimization). Make a content schedule and stick to it.

6. Incorporate Affiliate Links Naturally: When including affiliate links in your content, make sure they fit naturally.

Forced or irrelevant links can turn off your audience and make you seem untrustworthy.

7. Use Calls to Action (CTAs): Encourage your audience to take action, such as clicking on an affiliate link or subscribing to your email list, with clear and compelling CTAs.

8. Be Honest and Transparent: Always be honest and transparent about your affiliations. Disclose your affiliate links and be honest in your reviews and recommendations.

By creating valuable and relevant content, you can build a strong relationship with your audience, enhance your credibility, and increase your affiliate marketing success.

7.4 ENGAGING WITH YOUR AUDIENCE

Engaging with your audience is crucial for building trust, increasing loyalty, and fostering a sense of community. It makes your audience feel valued and heard, and it can provide valuable insights into their needs and preferences. Here's how you can effectively engage with your audience:

1. Be Active on Social Media: Social media is a powerful tool for engaging with your audience.

Share your content, ask questions, respond to comments, and participate in discussions. Be sure to choose the social media platforms that your audience uses most.

2. Encourage Comments and Feedback: Invite your audience to share their thoughts, experiences, and questions. This could be through blog comments, social media posts, or email. Always respond in a timely and respectful manner.

3. Create Interactive Content: Interactive content, such as quizzes, polls, or contests, can be a fun and engaging way to interact with your audience. It can also provide valuable data about your audience.

4. Host Webinars or Live Streams: Hosting webinars or live streams is a great way to interact with your audience in real time. You can share information, answer questions, and get instant feedback.

5. Personalize Your Communications: Personalizing your communications, such as using a person's name in emails or addressing their specific concerns, can make your audience feel special and valued.

6. Show Appreciation: Show appreciation for your audience's support and engagement. This could be through thank-you messages, shout-outs, or special offers.

7. Be Genuine and Authentic: Engage with your audience in a genuine and authentic manner. Avoid automated or generic responses. Let your personality shine through, and show your audience that there's a real person behind the brand.

Remember, engaging with your audience is not just about increasing your affiliate marketing success. It's also about building meaningful relationships and providing value. The more you engage with your audience, the more you'll understand them, and the better you can serve them.

8.1 SEO STRATEGIES FOR DRIVING TRAFFIC

Search Engine Optimization (SEO) is a powerful strategy to drive organic traffic to your affiliate links. When executed correctly, it can lead to a steady stream of visitors without the need for paid advertising.

Below are some key SEO strategies:

1. **Keyword Research:** This is the process of finding and analyzing the terms that people enter into search engines. Use tools like Google Keyword Planner, SEMrush, or Ahrefs to find keywords relevant to your niche and the products you're promoting. Consider both search volume and competitiveness.

2. **On-Page SEO:** This involves optimizing individual web pages on your site, including the content and the HTML source code. Use your keywords in strategic places like the title tag,

URL, headers, and throughout the content. But remember, don't stuff your content with keywords; it should read naturally.

3. **Quality Content:** Search engines favor high-quality, valuable content that meets users' needs.

Regularly publish unique, comprehensive content that provides value to your audience and incorporates your target keywords.

4. **Site Structure and Navigation:** A well-organized site with clear navigation helps search engines index your site and improves user experience. Include a sitemap and use internal linking to help search engines understand the structure and content of your site.

5. **Mobile Optimization:** With the majority of web browsing now happening on mobile devices, it's crucial that your website is mobile-friendly. This affects both your search engine rankings and user experience.

6. Speed Optimization: Page load speed is a ranking factor for search engines. A slow site can hurt your rankings and frustrate users. Use tools like Google PageSpeed Insights to check your site's speed and get recommendations for improvement.

7. Backlinks: Backlinks, or inbound links from other websites, signal to search engines that your content is valuable and trustworthy. To build backlinks, you can use strategies like guest posting, influencer outreach, and creating shareable content.

Remember, SEO is a long-term strategy. It takes time to see results, but it can be incredibly effective for driving traffic to your affiliate links. Stay up to date with the latest SEO trends and changes to search engine algorithms to keep your SEO strategy effective.

Social media is a powerful tool for driving traffic to your affiliate links. It allows you to reach a large audience, engage with potential customers, and direct them to your website or affiliate products.

Here's how you can leverage social media for traffic generation:

1. **Choose the Right Platforms:** Not all social media platforms are created equal. Each one has a unique audience and works best with certain types of content. Choose the platforms that align with your target audience and content strategy.

2. **Share Valuable Content:** The content you share on social media should be valuable to your audience. This could be your own content, such as blog posts or videos, or curated content from other reputable sources. Remember to incorporate your affiliate links naturally within your content.

3. Engage with Your Audience: Social media is all about engagement. Respond to comments, participate in discussions, and be active on the platforms. This will help you build relationships with your audience, which can lead to increased traffic.

4. Use Hashtags: Hashtags can help increase the visibility of your posts. Use relevant hashtags that your target audience is likely to search for. But don't overdo it - too many hashtags can look spammy.

5. Leverage Influencer Marketing: Influencers have large, engaged audiences that trust their recommendations. Collaborating with influencers in your niche can help you reach a larger audience and drive more traffic to your affiliate links.

6. Promote Your Social Media: Include links to your social media profiles on your website, in your email signature, and in

any other marketing materials. This will help you grow your social media audience and increase your reach.

7. Monitor and Adjust: Use analytics tools to monitor the performance of your social media marketing. Pay attention to which posts generate the most traffic, and adjust your strategy accordingly.

Remember, social media marketing is about building relationships and providing value. By being active, engaging, and consistent, you can use social media to drive significant traffic to your affiliate links.

8.3 PAY-PER-CLICK ADVERTISING FOR AFFILIATES

Pay-Per-Click (PPC) advertising can be an effective method for driving traffic to your affiliate links, especially when you want quick results. With PPC, you pay a fee each time one of your ads is clicked.

Here's how you can use PPC advertising in your affiliate marketing:

1. Choosing the Right Platform: There are various PPC platforms, but Google AdWords and Facebook Ads are among the most popular.

Choose the platform that aligns with your target audience. Some affiliate programs may have restrictions on PPC advertising, so be sure to check their terms.

2. Keyword Research: In PPC advertising, keywords are crucial. You bid on keywords related to your niche, so when people search for those terms, your ad can appear in the search results. Use keyword research tools to find relevant, high-traffic keywords with low competition.

3. Crafting Your Ad: Create compelling ad copy that grabs attention and prompts users to click. Make it clear what you're offering and what the benefits are. Use a strong call-to-action to encourage clicks.

4. Landing Page Optimization: When users click on your ad, they should be directed to a relevant and well-optimized landing page. This page should be relevant to your ad and offer a seamless experience. It should be easy to navigate, with a clear call-to-action and an easy way to make a purchase or take the desired action.

5. Testing and Adjusting: PPC advertising requires regular monitoring and adjustment. Test different keywords, ad copy, and landing pages to see what works best. Use the analytics provided by the PPC platform to make data-driven decisions.

6. Setting a Budget: Set a budget for your PPC campaign and stick to it. PPC can be costly, so it's important to ensure that your return on investment (ROI) makes it worthwhile.

Remember, while PPC can drive traffic quickly, it's not a replacement for organic traffic strategies. It should be used as part of a comprehensive marketing strategy that includes SEO, content marketing, and social media.

Guest blogging, and other similar strategies, are effective ways to drive traffic to your affiliate links, build your online presence, and establish authority in your niche.

Here's how you can leverage these strategies:

1. Guest Blogging: Guest blogging involves writing a blog post to be published on another website.

This can help you reach a larger audience, build backlinks, and drive traffic back to your website. Reach out to reputable blogs in your niche, and propose a high-quality, relevant blog post. Include your affiliate links subtly and naturally in your content.

2. Collaborations and Partnerships: Collaborating with other businesses or influencers in your niche can help you reach a larger audience. This could involve joint webinars, social media takeovers, or shared promotions. Make sure to choose partners whose audience aligns with your target market.

3. Forums and Community Engagement: Participating in online forums and communities relevant to your niche can help you build authority and drive traffic to your affiliate links. Sites like Reddit, Quora, or niche-specific forums are good places to start. Remember to provide value first, answer questions, and share your links only when relevant and allowed by the community rules.

4. Email Marketing: Building an email list and regularly sending out valuable content can be an effective way to drive consistent traffic to your affiliate links.

You can include your affiliate links in your newsletters, but ensure the primary focus is on delivering value to your subscribers.

5. Video Marketing: Platforms like YouTube are becoming increasingly popular. Creating video content related to your niche and including your affiliate links in the video description can be an effective way to drive traffic.

6. Podcasting: If you have a podcast, or are a guest on someone else's podcast, this can be a great opportunity to share your affiliate links. Talk about products or services that you're an affiliate for in a natural, conversational way.

Remember, the key to all these strategies is to provide value first. Aim to build trust and relationships, rather than just promoting your affiliate links. By offering value, you'll build credibility and increase the chances of your audience clicking on your affiliate links.

9.1 UNDERSTANDING CONVERSION RATE OPTIMIZATION

Conversion Rate Optimization (CRO) is the process of increasing the percentage of your website visitors who take a desired action, like clicking on an affiliate link, signing up for a newsletter, or making a purchase. Understanding and implementing CRO strategies is key to making the most out of your affiliate marketing efforts.

Here's an overview of CRO:

1. **Importance of CRO:** Without effective CRO, even the highest-traffic website won't lead to sales. It's not enough to get people to visit your site; you need to persuade them to take action. Effective CRO means more conversions, which translates into more sales with the same amount of traffic.

2. **Understanding Your Audience:** CRO starts with understanding your audience. What are their needs,

preferences, and pain points? What motivates them to take action? Use methods like audience research, surveys, and user testing to gain insights.

3. **Designing for Conversions:** How your website is designed can significantly impact your conversion rate. Clear navigation, professional design, fast load times, and mobile optimization all contribute to better user experience and higher conversions.

4. **Crafting Compelling Calls to Action:** A call to action (CTA) prompts your visitors to take a specific action. Your CTAs should be clear, compelling, and prominently placed on your page.

5. **Testing and Improvement:** CRO is a continuous process of testing, analyzing, and refining. Use A/B testing to compare different elements of your site and see what leads to higher conversions. Make adjustments based on data, not assumptions.

6. Analyzing Performance: Use analytics tools to track your conversion rate and other key metrics. This will give you insights into how your CRO efforts are performing and where there's room for improvement.

By understanding and implementing CRO, you can maximize your affiliate marketing earnings and ensure that your efforts in driving traffic to your site aren't wasted.

9.2 CRAFTING EFFECTIVE CALLS TO ACTION

An effective Call to Action (CTA) can significantly increase conversions by compelling your visitors to take the desired action. Here's how you can craft effective CTAs for your affiliate marketing efforts:

1. Make it Action-Oriented: Your CTA should use strong, action-oriented verbs. For instance, instead of saying "Our Newsletter", say "Subscribe to Our Newsletter". This directs the reader towards a specific action.

2. Create a Sense of Urgency: Creating a sense of urgency can encourage your audience to act immediately, rather than putting it off and potentially forgetting. Use phrases like "Limited Time Offer", "Offer Ends Soon", or "Only a Few Left" to prompt quick action.

3. Clearly Communicate the Benefit: Your audience should know exactly what they'll get by taking action. Ensure that the benefit is clear and compelling. For example, instead of just "Download Now", you might say "Download Your Free Guide to Affiliate Marketing".

4. Make it Stand Out: Your CTA should be visually striking and easy to find on the page. Use contrasting colors, large text, and ample white space around the CTA to make it stand out.

5. Keep it Simple: Don't confuse your audience with too many choices. If you present too many CTAs at once, your audience might suffer from decision paralysis and end up not taking any action. Focus on one primary action you want users to take.

6. Test and Optimize: Test different CTAs to see what works best with your audience. You can test different text, colors, sizes, placements, and more. Use the data from these tests to continually optimize your CTAs.

Remember, an effective CTA can make the difference between a visitor simply leaving your site and a visitor turning into a customer. Spend time crafting your CTAs and testing them to ensure they're as effective as possible.

Landing pages play a crucial role in converting your website visitors into customers or leads. They're the place where you send your traffic, with the aim of persuading visitors to take a particular action, such as buying a product or signing up for a newsletter.

Here's how you can create landing pages that convert:

1. Clear and Compelling Headline: The headline is the first thing visitors see when they land on your page, so it should be clear, compelling, and relevant to what you're offering.

2. Persuasive Copy: The content on your landing page should be persuasive and focused on the benefits of the product or service you're promoting. Use bullet points, headers, and short paragraphs to make your copy easy to read.

3. Visual Appeal: Visual elements like images, videos, infographics can significantly increase engagement and conversions. Ensure that these elements are high quality, relevant, and help illustrate the value of what you're offering.

4. Trust Signals: Testimonials, reviews, case studies, or security badges can help build trust and reassure visitors that your offer is reliable.

5. Clear Call-to-Action (CTA): Your CTA should be prominent and persuasive, telling visitors exactly what they should do next. It should be visually distinctive and placed in an easy-to-find location.

6. Minimal Distractions: Avoid including anything on your landing page that isn't relevant to the action you want visitors to take. This includes unnecessary links, complex navigation, or irrelevant information.

7. Mobile Optimization: With more and more people using mobile devices, it's critical that your landing page is optimized for mobile. It should load quickly and be easy to navigate on a small screen.

8. Testing and Optimization: Always test different versions of your landing page to see what works best. This could include testing different headlines, images, copy, or CTAs. Use this data to continually optimize your landing page.

By carefully designing and optimizing your landing pages, you can significantly increase your conversions and make the most of your affiliate marketing efforts.

9.4 TESTING AND OPTIMIZING FOR CONVERSIONS

Testing and optimization are critical for maximizing your affiliate marketing conversions. This process involves making data-driven changes to your strategies based on what works best with your audience. Here's how you can test and optimize your efforts for better conversions:

1. A/B Testing: Also known as split testing, A/B testing involves comparing two versions of a webpage, email, or other marketing element to see which performs better. For example, you might test two different calls to action, two different landing page designs, or two different headlines. The version that results in more conversions is the one you should use.

2. Analyze Your Metrics: Use tools like Google Analytics to track your key performance indicators (KPIs), such as conversion rate, bounce rate, and time on page.

This data can give you insights into what's working and what's not. For example, if you have a high bounce rate, it could indicate that your landing page isn't appealing or relevant to visitors.

3. User Experience Testing: User experience (UX) plays a big role in conversions. If your website is difficult to navigate, slow to load, or unappealing visually, it could deter visitors from converting. Use UX testing tools to get insights into how users interact with your site and where potential issues might lie.

4. Optimize for Mobile: More and more people are using mobile devices to browse the web, so it's critical that your website and landing pages are optimized for mobile. This means

ensuring they load quickly, are easy to navigate on a small screen, and offer a seamless experience across devices.

5. Continual Improvement: Conversion optimization isn't a one-time thing. It should be an ongoing process of testing, analyzing, and improving. As you learn more about your audience and as trends and technologies evolve, you should continually adjust your strategies to improve conversions.

Remember, the goal of testing and optimization is to make the most of the traffic you're getting. Even small improvements in your conversion rate can significantly increase your affiliate marketing earnings.

10.1 IMPLEMENTING SALES FUNNELS IN AFFILIATE MARKETING

A sales funnel is a step-by-step process that guides potential customers from the first time they learn about your product to the ultimate purchase. It's called a "funnel" because it starts broad (awareness) and narrows down (conversion). Using sales funnels can significantly enhance your affiliate marketing efforts.

Here's how:

1. Understanding the Sales Funnel Stages:

- Awareness: The potential customer becomes aware of your product or service. In affiliate marketing, this could be through your blog post, social media content, or email newsletter.

- Interest: The potential customer starts to research and compare different options. They might read reviews, look at product comparisons, or read more in-depth content about the product.

- Decision: The potential customer decides they're ready to make a purchase. They've chosen the product they want to buy and are looking for the best place or offer to purchase it.

- Action: The potential customer makes the purchase, hopefully through your affiliate link.

2. Creating Content for Each Stage: Create different types of content to target potential customers at each stage of the funnel. For example, a blog post could raise awareness, a detailed product review could generate interest, and an exclusive discount code could help drive the decision.

3. Leveraging Email Marketing: Email marketing can be a powerful tool for guiding potential customers through your sales funnel. You can send regular emails providing value and subtly promoting your affiliate products.

4. Retargeting and Follow Up: Not all potential customers will make a purchase the first time they come across your affiliate link. Retargeting ads and follow-up emails can help remind them of the product and give them additional reasons to make the purchase.

5. Analyzing and Optimizing Your Funnel: Use analytics tools to understand where potential customers are dropping off in your funnel. Then, make changes to your content, offers, or marketing strategies to improve these areas.

By implementing a sales funnel in your affiliate marketing strategy, you can guide potential customers toward making a purchase, rather than hoping they'll stumble upon your affiliate link and decide to buy.

10.2 RETARGETING STRATEGIES FOR AFFILIATES

Retargeting, also known as remarketing, is a form of online advertising that helps you keep your brand in front of bounced traffic after they leave your website.

Here's how you can implement retargeting strategies as an affiliate:

1. Understand the Basics of Retargeting: Retargeting works by placing a small piece of code on your website (often called a pixel). This code leaves a cookie in your visitors' browsers, allowing you to serve them targeted ads as they browse elsewhere on the web.

2. Segment Your Audience: Not all visitors to your site are the same. Some might be at the awareness stage, while others are closer to making a purchase. Segment your audience based on their behavior on your site and target them with personalized ads.

3. Tailor Your Ads: Retargeting is most effective when the ads are tailored to the audience. For example, if a visitor left a product review page without clicking on your affiliate link, you could retarget them with an ad for that product, possibly offering a special discount or highlighting the benefits of the product.

4. Leverage Different Platforms: Different retargeting platforms offer different benefits. For example, Google Ads reach a vast network of sites, while Facebook allows for more precise demographic and interest targeting.

5. Set the Right Frequency: It's important to set the right frequency for your retargeting ads. Too few, and you may not make an impact; too many, and you might annoy your audience.

6. Test and Optimize: Like all marketing strategies, it's crucial to test different elements of your retargeting campaign and optimize based on your results. This could include trying different ad creatives, targeting parameters, and ad placements.

Remember, the primary aim of retargeting is to attract individuals who have already shown an interest in your affiliate products.

By reminding them of what they've viewed or nudging them with a tempting offer, you're likely to increase your conversion rate.

Automating certain tasks can help streamline your affiliate marketing business, making it more efficient and freeing up your time for more high-value activities.

Here's how you can go about it:

1. Email Marketing Automation: Automating your email marketing can save a lot of time. You can create automated email sequences for new subscribers, set up automatic replies, and schedule your newsletters in advance.

Tools like MailChimp, Constant Contact, or ConvertKit can help with this.

2. Social Media Automation: Posting consistently on social media can be time-consuming. Automation tools like Buffer or

Hootsuite allow you to schedule your posts in advance and manage all your social media accounts from one place.

3. Content Creation Automation: While you can't entirely automate content creation, certain tools can help streamline the process. For example, you can use AI-powered writing tools for content ideas or outline generation, or graphic design tools like Canva for easy and fast visual content creation.

4. Affiliate Marketing Tools: There are various tools designed specifically for affiliate marketers. These can automate tasks like link tracking, reporting, and commission payouts. Examples include ClickBank, CJ Affiliate, and Voluum.

5. Customer Relationship Management (CRM): CRMs help manage your interactions with current and potential customers. By automating CRM processes, you can ensure that no leads fall through the cracks and that you're always nurturing your customer relationships.

6. Data Analysis and Reporting: Use tools like Google Analytics or SEMrush to automate data collection and reporting. These platforms can provide you with valuable insights into your website traffic, SEO performance, and more.

Automation can be a major game-changer in your affiliate marketing business.

It's important to remember, however, that automation should complement your efforts, not replace them. There's no substitute for personal touches and high-quality, unique content.

10.4 EXPLORING MULTI-TIER AFFILIATE MARKETING

Multi-tier affiliate marketing is a strategy where affiliates can earn commissions on the sales or referrals made by other affiliates that they've recruited. This approach can exponentially increase your earning potential if done correctly. Here's how to explore multi-tier affiliate marketing:

1. Understand the Different Tiers: In a two-tier affiliate program, you earn a commission on your direct sales or referrals (first tier) and on the sales or referrals made by affiliates you've recruited (second tier). Some programs may offer additional tiers, allowing you to earn from further levels of affiliates recruited by your first-tier affiliates.

2. Choose the Right Program: Not all affiliate programs offer multi-tier commissions.

You'll need to research and choose programs that offer this opportunity. Ensure these programs also have high-quality products or services, as you'll be recommending both the affiliate program and the products to others.

3. Recruit Affiliates: To earn from multi-tier affiliate marketing, you'll need to recruit other affiliates. This could involve promoting the affiliate program on your website or through your email list, leveraging your professional network, or using social media.

4. Support Your Affiliates: To increase the chances of your recruited affiliates making sales (and therefore earning you commissions), you should provide them with support and training. This could include giving them tips on affiliate marketing, sharing successful marketing strategies, or providing them with promotional materials.

5. Track Your Earnings: Use the tracking tools provided by the affiliate program to monitor your earnings from different tiers. This can help you understand how effective your multi-tier strategy is and where to focus your efforts.

Remember, while multi-tier affiliate marketing can increase your earning potential, it also requires more work and strategic planning. You'll need to effectively promote the affiliate program, recruit motivated affiliates, and provide them with ongoing support to increase their sales.

11.1 TOOLS AND TECHNIQUES FOR TRACKING SUCCESS

In affiliate marketing, understanding your performance is essential to refine your strategies and maximize your earnings. Here are some key tools and techniques for tracking your success:

1. **Affiliate Marketing Dashboards:** Most affiliate programs provide dashboards where you can monitor your earnings, click-through rates, conversion rates, and other key metrics. These dashboards are a great starting point for understanding your performance.

2. Google Analytics: Google Analytics is a free and powerful tool for understanding your website's traffic. You can track which pages your visitors are coming from, what pages they're visiting on your site, how long they're staying, and other key

data. By setting up goal tracking, you can even monitor how many users are clicking on your affiliate links.

3. Heatmap Tools: Heatmap tools, like Hotjar or Crazy Egg, provide a visual representation of how visitors interact with your website. They can show you where users are clicking, how far they're scrolling, and what areas of your site are getting the most attention. This information can help you optimize your site's layout and understand where best to place your affiliate links.

4. A/B Testing Tools: A/B testing tools, like Optimizely or Google Optimize, allow you to test two versions of a webpage to see which performs better. You could test different placements of your affiliate links, different calls to action, or different landing page designs.

5. Social Media Analytics: If you're promoting your affiliate links on social media, don't overlook the analytics offered by

these platforms. They can provide insights into your post engagement, audience demographics, and best times to post.

6. Email Marketing Analytics: If you're using email marketing, tools like MailChimp or ConvertKit provide detailed analytics on open rates, click-through rates, and conversions. These insights can help you optimize your email marketing strategy.

The goal of tracking your success is to understand what's working and what's not, so you can adjust your strategies accordingly. Regularly review your metrics, experiment with different tactics, and continually optimize your efforts for better results.

11.2 INTERPRETING AND ANALYZING PERFORMANCE DATA

Interpreting and analyzing performance data is crucial for understanding the effectiveness of your affiliate marketing strategies and making data-driven decisions to improve them. Here are some key steps:

1. Set Clear Goals: Before diving into data analysis, you need to establish clear, measurable goals. Are you aiming to increase traffic, improve conversion rates, or perhaps boost engagement on your content? Having clear goals helps you focus your analysis on the metrics that matter most.

2. Understand Key Metrics: Here are some key metrics to consider:

- Traffic: The number of visitors to your website or landing page.

- Click-Through Rate (CTR): The percentage of your audience that clicks on your affiliate links.

- Conversion Rate: The percentage of visitors who click on your affiliate links and make a purchase.

- Average Order Value (AOV): The average amount spent each time a customer places an order.

- Earnings Per Click (EPC): The average amount you earn each time someone clicks on your affiliate link.

3. Analyze Trends: Look for trends in your data. Is your traffic or conversion rate increasing or decreasing over time? Are there certain times of the day, week, or year when you see peaks in performance?

4. Segment Your Data: Segment your data to gain more detailed insights. For example, you could segment by traffic source to see whether visitors from search engines, social media, or email marketing are more likely to click on your affiliate links.

5. Compare Performance Across Different Campaigns: If you're promoting multiple affiliate products or running different marketing campaigns, compare their performance.

This can help you understand what types of products or marketing strategies are most effective for your audience.

6. Test and Optimize: Use your data to experiment with different strategies, test new ideas, and optimize your marketing efforts. For example, if you find that your CTR is low,

you could try changing the placement of your affiliate links or the wording of your calls to action. The goal of data analysis is to gain insights that can help you improve your affiliate marketing strategies. Don't be afraid to dive deep into your data, ask critical questions, and continuously strive for improvement.

11.3 ADJUSTING STRATEGIES BASED ON PERFORMANCE

After interpreting and analyzing your performance data, the next step is to adjust your strategies accordingly.

Here's how to go about it:

1. **Identify Strengths and Weaknesses:** Firstly, identify which of your strategies are working well and which are not. This involves identifying trends, anomalies, and patterns in your performance data.

2. **Experiment with New Approaches:** If certain aspects of your strategy aren't working as well as you'd like, consider

testing new approaches. This might involve trying different marketing channels, varying the types of content you produce, or experimenting with different calls to action.

3. Enhance Successful Strategies: Conversely, if certain strategies are working well, consider how you can further enhance them. Could you invest more in your successful PPC campaigns? Could you expand your most popular content types or topics?

4. Reassess Your Audience: Performance data can also provide insights into your audience's behavior and preferences. If certain products or content types are particularly successful, this could indicate what your audience is most interested in or what problems they're looking to solve.

5. Test, Analyze, Optimize, Repeat: Performance data isn't just a one-time thing; it's something you should continually monitor and learn from. Regularly review your performance, test new strategies, analyze the results, and optimize based on your findings.

6. Be Patient: Finally, remember that seeing the results of changes can take time. It's important to allow enough time for changes to take effect before deciding on their success or failure.

By adjusting your strategies based on performance, you're not just guessing or assuming what works - you're making data-driven decisions, which is a powerful way to maximize your success in affiliate marketing.

11.4 MANAGING MULTIPLE AFFILIATE PROGRAMS

Managing multiple affiliate programs can be a challenging task, but with the right approach, it can also significantly diversify your income sources.

Here are some tips to effectively manage multiple affiliate programs:

1. Stay Organized: With multiple programs to manage, keeping track of your accounts, links, payments, and performance data can be complex. Use spreadsheets or specialized affiliate management tools to keep everything organized.

2. Understand Each Program: Different affiliate programs can have different commission structures, payment terms, and rules. Make sure you fully understand each program you're participating in and adjust your strategies accordingly.

3. Prioritize Your Efforts: You may not be able to give equal attention to all programs. Prioritize your efforts based on the potential return of each program. Programs with higher commissions, higher conversion rates, or products that are more relevant to your audience may deserve more of your attention.

4. Diversify but Don't Overstretch: While participating in multiple programs can diversify your income, trying to promote too many can dilute your efforts and confuse your audience. Only promote products that are relevant to your audience and provide real value.

5. Monitor Performance: Regularly check the performance of each affiliate program. If a particular program isn't delivering satisfactory results, consider whether it's worth the effort you're putting into it.

6. Provide Distinct Value for Each Product: Ensure that you are providing unique and useful content for each product you are promoting. This will help you to engage with different segments of your audience and increase the chances of conversions.

7. Maintain Ethical Standards: Promote only those products or services that you genuinely believe in. This not only maintains your credibility with your audience but also complies with most affiliate programs' terms of service. Managing multiple affiliate programs should not compromise the quality of your content or your relationship with your audience. Always aim for a balance between diversifying your income and providing real value to your audience.

12.1 UNDERSTANDING LEGAL OBLIGATIONS

In affiliate marketing, just as in any other business, it's important to understand and adhere to your legal obligations. Here are key legal aspects to consider:

1. Disclosure: According to the guidelines set by the Federal Trade Commission (FTC) in the United States and similar bodies in other countries, it's necessary to disclose your affiliate relationship. This means that if you're promoting a product and receive a commission on sales, you must clearly inform your audience of this fact. The disclosure should be clear, conspicuous, and close to your affiliate links.

2. Privacy Policies and Cookie Laws: If you're collecting user data on your website (like email addresses for a newsletter), you must have a privacy policy in place that tells your visitors what information you collect and how you use it.

If you're using cookies, particularly for tracking affiliate sales, you may also need to inform your visitors and get their consent, according to laws like the EU's General Data Protection Regulation (GDPR) and ePrivacy Directive.

3. Advertising Standards: Any claims you make about a product, such as its performance or results, must be truthful and you should be able to back them up. Exaggerating or misleading your audience can lead to legal issues.

4. Trademark Laws: When promoting a product, be careful not to infringe on the company's trademarks. This includes unauthorized use of logos or making it appear as if you're part of the company when you're actually an independent affiliate.

5. Tax Obligations: Income earned from affiliate marketing is taxable, so you need to keep accurate records of your earnings and expenses. The exact procedures and rates will depend on your local tax laws and your personal situation, so consider getting advice from a tax professional.

Remember, these are general guidelines and legal requirements can vary by country, so it's always a good idea to get legal advice for your specific situation. Adhering to these legal obligations not only keeps you on the right side of the law but also helps maintain trust with your audience.

12.2 FOLLOWING FTC GUIDELINES FOR AFFILIATES

The Federal Trade Commission (FTC) in the United States has established guidelines to ensure transparency and fairness in affiliate marketing. As an affiliate marketer, it's important to follow these guidelines to maintain trust with your audience and comply with legal requirements.

Here's an overview of the key FTC guidelines for affiliates:

1. Disclosure of Affiliate Relationships: Disclose your affiliate relationships clearly and conspicuously. The disclosure should be placed close to the affiliate links or recommendations, making it easily noticeable and understandable to your audience. Avoid ambiguous language and ensure that your disclosure is transparent about your financial interests.

2. Clear and Unambiguous Statements: When endorsing a product or making a claim about its benefits, ensure that your statements are accurate, truthful, and not misleading. Avoid exaggerations, false promises, or deceptive practices that can mislead your audience.

3. Genuine Recommendations: Your recommendations should be based on genuine experiences and beliefs. Don't endorse products solely for financial gain without truly believing in their value or relevance to your audience. Maintaining integrity and providing authentic recommendations is essential for building trust.

4. Unbiased Reviews and Opinions: If you provide product reviews or comparisons, make sure they are unbiased and based on objective criteria. Disclose any biases, conflicts of interest, or free products you may have received for reviewing purposes.

5. Endorsements and Testimonials: If you use endorsements or testimonials from individuals, ensure that they reflect genuine experiences and results. Disclose any material connections or compensation involved in obtaining those endorsements.

6. Compliance with Other Laws and Regulations: In addition to FTC guidelines, ensure compliance with other relevant laws and regulations, such as data protection laws (e.g., GDPR), advertising standards, and trademark laws. Understand the specific requirements in your country or region and adhere to them.

It's essential to stay updated on FTC guidelines and any amendments or updates that may be issued. By following these guidelines, you not only comply with legal obligations but also build credibility and trust with your audience, leading to long-term success in affiliate marketing.

Ethics play a vital role in affiliate marketing. Upholding ethical standards ensures transparency, credibility, and a positive reputation among your audience.

Here are some key ethical considerations to keep in mind:

1. Honesty and Transparency: Be honest and transparent with your audience. Disclose your affiliate relationships and any financial incentives you receive from promoting products or services. Clearly communicate that your recommendations are based on your own assessment and experience.

2. Authenticity and Integrity: Promote products or services that you genuinely believe in and that align with your values. Don't compromise your integrity by endorsing products solely for financial gain. Authenticity is crucial for building trust with your audience.

3. Providing Value and Accuracy: Ensure that your content provides genuine value to your audience. Offer accurate information, unbiased reviews, and helpful insights. Misleading or deceptive practices can harm your reputation and the trust you've built.

4. Audience-Centric Approach: Put your audience's best interests first. Understand their needs, preferences, and challenges. Tailor your recommendations to genuinely address their concerns and provide solutions that benefit them.

5. Quality Content Creation: Create high-quality, informative, and engaging content that adds value to your audience's lives. Aim to educate, inspire, and help them make informed decisions. Avoid spammy or low-quality content that solely focuses on making sales.

6. Ethical Advertising Practices: Follow ethical advertising practices by complying with advertising guidelines and regulations. Avoid deceptive tactics, false claims, or manipulative strategies that mislead or exploit your audience.

7. Respect for Privacy and Data Protection: Respect your audience's privacy and adhere to data protection laws and regulations. Safeguard their personal information and be transparent about how you collect, use, and protect their data.

8. Responsible Affiliate Partner Selection: Choose affiliate partners that are reputable, offer quality products or services, and have ethical business practices. Research and assess their track record, customer reviews, and overall reputation before entering into partnerships.

By adhering to these ethical considerations, you build a strong foundation of trust with your audience. Prioritize the long-term relationship with your audience over short-term gains, and strive to make a positive impact through your affiliate marketing endeavors.

12.4 MANAGING DISPUTES AND ISSUES

While affiliate marketing can be a rewarding endeavor, there may be instances where disputes or issues arise.

Here are some tips for effectively managing and resolving conflicts:

1. Communication and Professionalism: Maintain open and professional communication with all parties involved. Be respectful and avoid confrontational or aggressive behavior. Clearly express your concerns or issues and listen to the other party's perspective.

2. Review Affiliate Program Terms and Policies: Familiarize yourself with the terms and policies of the affiliate programs you participate in. Understand the guidelines for dispute resolution, payment disputes, or any other issues that may arise. If a conflict occurs, refer to these guidelines to understand your rights and responsibilities.

3. Document Everything: Keep a record of all interactions, agreements, and important communications related to the dispute. This includes emails, screenshots, contracts, invoices, or any other relevant documents. Documentation will help support your case if formal action needs to be taken.

4. Seek Resolution Through Direct Communication: Initially, try to resolve the dispute through direct communication with the involved parties. Discuss the issue calmly and attempt to find a mutually agreeable solution. Often, misunderstandings or miscommunications can be resolved amicably through open dialogue.

5. Mediation or Arbitration: If direct communication doesn't lead to a satisfactory resolution, consider seeking mediation or arbitration. These processes involve a neutral third party who can facilitate discussions and help reach a fair agreement. Many affiliate programs have dispute resolution mechanisms in place to assist with these situations.

6. Legal Advice: In certain cases, you may need to seek legal advice, especially if the dispute involves significant financial implications or contractual breaches. Consult with an attorney who specializes in affiliate marketing or contract law to understand your rights and options.

7. Protect Your Reputation: Throughout the dispute resolution process, maintain professionalism and protect your reputation. Refrain from making defamatory statements or engaging in public disputes that could harm your credibility. Focus on finding a resolution while preserving your professional image.

While disputes and issues can be challenging, approaching them with a proactive and professional mindset can lead to satisfactory resolutions. Prioritize open communication, seek assistance when necessary, and protect your long-term relationships and reputation in the affiliate marketing industry.

13.1 AFFILIATE MARKETING ON BLOGS

Blogs are a popular platform for affiliate marketing due to their ability to provide in-depth content, engage with audiences, and establish a loyal following.

Here's how to effectively leverage affiliate marketing on blogs:

1. Choose the Right Niche: Select a niche that aligns with your interests, expertise, and audience's needs. Focusing on a specific niche allows you to become an authority and build credibility in that area.

2. Quality Content Creation: Create high-quality, valuable, and engaging content that resonates with your audience. Offer informative articles, tutorials, product reviews, and comparisons. Incorporate your affiliate links strategically within the content.

3. Disclose Affiliate Relationships: Disclose your affiliate relationships clearly and conspicuously in compliance with FTC guidelines. Place a disclosure statement on your blog to ensure transparency with your audience.

4. Build an Engaged Audience: Focus on building a loyal and engaged audience. Encourage comments, respond to questions, and foster community engagement. By establishing a connection with your readers, you increase the likelihood of them trusting and acting upon your recommendations.

5. Targeted Promotion and Link Placement: Identify the most effective ways to promote affiliate products within your content. Consider using product comparison tables, call-to-action buttons, or highlighting special discounts or promotions. Experiment with different link placements and track their performance.

6. Utilize Email Marketing: Leverage email marketing to nurture relationships with your audience. Provide valuable content through newsletters and include affiliate promotions when relevant. Segment your email list to tailor recommendations based on subscribers' interests.

7. Optimize for SEO: Implement effective search engine optimization (SEO) strategies to increase your blog's visibility in search results. Conduct keyword research, optimize meta tags, and create valuable content that aligns with search intent. Higher visibility can attract more organic traffic and potential customers.

8. Monitor Performance and Analyze Data: Regularly analyze your blog's performance using tools like Google Analytics. Track key metrics such as traffic, click-through rates, conversion rates, and earnings per click. Use this data to optimize your strategies and improve your results. Remember, success in affiliate marketing on blogs requires a long-term approach. Focus on building trust, providing value, and engaging with your audience. By consistently delivering

high-quality content and strategic affiliate promotions, you can maximize your earnings and establish yourself as a trusted affiliate marketer within your niche.

YouTube is a powerful platform for affiliate marketing, as it allows you to engage with a vast audience through video content. Here's how you can effectively leverage YouTube for affiliate marketing:

1. Choose a Niche and Target Audience: Select a niche that aligns with your interests and expertise. Identify your target audience and create content that caters to their needs and preferences.

2. Provide Valuable Content: Create high-quality videos that offer value to your viewers. Provide informative tutorials, product reviews, demonstrations, or helpful tips related to your niche. Demonstrate your expertise and build trust with your audience.

3. Incorporate Affiliate Links Strategically: Include your affiliate links in video descriptions, annotations, or as part of your video content. Clearly explain the benefits of the products or services you're promoting and how they can solve your audience's problems.

4. Be Transparent and Disclose Affiliate Relationships: Adhere to FTC guidelines by disclosing your affiliate relationships. Clearly state that you may earn a commission if viewers make a purchase through your affiliate links. Include this disclosure in video descriptions or verbally mention it in your videos.

5. Engage with Your Audience: Interact with your viewers by responding to comments, asking for feedback, and encouraging discussion. Engaging with your audience strengthens your connection, builds trust, and encourages them to take action on your recommendations.

6. Collaborate with Brands and Other Influencers:

Collaborate with brands or other influencers in your niche. Partnering with relevant brands can provide unique affiliate opportunities and expand your reach to new audiences. Just ensure that the collaborations align with your values and resonate with your audience.

7. Optimize Video Titles, Descriptions, and Tags:

Implement search engine optimization (SEO) strategies for your videos. Use relevant keywords in your video titles, descriptions, and tags to improve visibility in YouTube search results. This helps attract organic traffic to your videos.

8. Analyze Performance Metrics: Regularly review and

analyze your YouTube analytics to understand your video performance, audience demographics, watch time, and engagement. Identify trends, assess the success of different videos, and optimize your content based on the data. Remember, building a successful YouTube channel takes time and consistent effort. Focus on delivering valuable content, engaging with your audience, and strategically promoting affiliate products. By creating a loyal following and maintaining transparency, you can maximize your affiliate marketing success on YouTube.

13.3 LEVERAGING INSTAGRAM FOR AFFILIATE PROFITS

Instagram is a visual platform that offers immense potential for affiliate marketing. With its focus on engaging imagery and storytelling, you can effectively promote affiliate products to your audience. Here's how to leverage Instagram for affiliate profits:

1. Choose a Targeted Niche: Identify a niche that aligns with your interests, expertise, and audience preferences. Focusing on a specific niche allows you to build a dedicated following and establish yourself as an authority.

2. Build an Engaged Following: Create a visually appealing and cohesive Instagram feed. Post high-quality images and videos that resonate with your target audience. Engage with

your followers by responding to comments, asking questions, and fostering meaningful conversations.

3. **Provide Valuable and Authentic Content:** Create content that provides value and showcases the benefits of the products or services you're promoting. Be authentic and genuine in your recommendations, ensuring they align with your audience's interests and needs.

4. **Craft Compelling Captions:** Write engaging captions that tell a story, evoke emotions, or provide insights related to the affiliate products. Include your affiliate links strategically in your captions, ensuring they're easily clickable and trackable.

5. **Utilize Instagram Stories and Live Videos:** Leverage Instagram Stories and live videos to engage with your audience in real-time.

Share behind-the-scenes content, product demonstrations, or exclusive promotions. Use interactive features like polls, quizzes, or question stickers to encourage audience participation.

6. Collaborate with Brands and Influencers: Partner with brands and collaborate with influencers in your niche. These partnerships can lead to sponsored content or unique affiliate opportunities. Ensure that collaborations align with your audience's interests and maintain transparency about any paid partnerships.

7. Engage with Your Audience: Respond to comments, direct messages, and engage with your followers on a personal level. Show appreciation for their support and make them feel valued. Building a strong connection with your audience can lead to higher engagement and conversions.

8. Track Performance and Optimize: Regularly analyze your Instagram insights to track the performance of your posts, story views, engagement rates, and audience demographics. Identify which content performs best and optimize your

strategy accordingly. Test different approaches, such as posting times, content formats, or promotional techniques, to refine your affiliate marketing efforts. Remember, Instagram is a visually driven platform, so focus on creating eye-catching content that resonates with your audience. Be consistent, authentic, and build trust with your followers. By effectively leveraging Instagram, you can generate affiliate profits while nurturing a loyal and engaged community.

13.4 OTHER PLATFORMS: TIKTOK, LINKEDIN, PODCASTS

Affiliate marketing extends beyond traditional platforms like blogs, YouTube, and Instagram. Here's how you can leverage other platforms for affiliate marketing success:

1. TikTok: Identify trends and challenges relevant to your niche and create short, engaging videos that incorporate affiliate promotions.

Utilize TikTok's features like duets, stitches, and challenges to collaborate with other creators and increase your reach.

Include a clear call-to-action in your videos and use the link in your bio to direct followers to your affiliate offers.

2. LinkedIn: Share informative articles, videos, or thought leadership content related to your niche on LinkedIn.

Engage in relevant industry groups and contribute valuable insights, positioning yourself as an authority.

Leverage LinkedIn's publishing platform to create long-form content and incorporate affiliate links where appropriate.

3. Podcasts: Start a podcast focused on your niche and provide valuable, in-depth discussions or interviews.

Incorporate affiliate links in your podcast episodes by verbally promoting products or including them in episode descriptions. Seek sponsorships or partnerships with relevant brands, offering affiliate promotions to your podcast listeners. Remember, when exploring different platforms, adapt your affiliate marketing strategies to fit the platform's unique format and audience. Maintain transparency, deliver value, and engage with your audience authentically. Continuously analyze your performance and optimize your approach based on the platform's metrics and feedback from your audience. With the right strategies, you can effectively monetize your affiliate marketing efforts across a variety of platforms.

14.1 OUTSOURCING TASKS AND PROCESSES

As your affiliate marketing business grows, you may find it beneficial to outsource certain tasks and processes. Outsourcing can help you focus on core activities, increase efficiency, and expand your business. Here's how to effectively outsource tasks and processes:

1. Identify Tasks for Outsourcing: Identify the tasks that consume a significant amount of your time or require specialized skills.

These could include content creation, graphic design, website maintenance, customer support, or data analysis.

2. Determine Your Budget: Establish a budget for outsourcing. Consider the value that outsourcing will bring to your business and allocate resources accordingly. Start small and gradually increase your outsourcing efforts as your revenue grows.

3. Find Reliable Freelancers or Agencies: Search for reliable freelancers or agencies that specialize in the tasks you want to outsource.

Platforms like Upwork, Fiverr, or Freelancer.com can help you connect with qualified professionals. Look for experience, expertise, and positive reviews.

4. Clearly Define Expectations: Clearly communicate your expectations, deliverables, timelines, and quality standards to the freelancers or agencies you hire. Provide detailed instructions and guidelines to ensure they understand your requirements.

5. Establish Effective Communication Channels: Set up efficient communication channels with your freelancers or agencies. Use project management tools like Asana, Trello, or Slack to collaborate, share files, and track progress. Schedule regular check-ins to address any questions or concerns.

6. Monitor Progress and Provide Feedback: Regularly monitor the progress of the outsourced tasks. Provide constructive feedback to freelancers or agencies to ensure alignment with your expectations. Encourage open communication and address any issues promptly.

7. Protect Confidentiality and Data Security: If you're sharing sensitive information or data with freelancers or agencies, ensure you have non-disclosure agreements (NDAs) in place. Implement data security measures to protect your business and your customers' information.

8. Evaluate and Adjust: Regularly evaluate the effectiveness of outsourcing efforts. Assess the impact on your business's growth, efficiency, and profitability. Adjust your outsourcing strategy as needed to optimize results. By outsourcing tasks and processes, you can focus on strategic activities that drive growth and revenue. Leverage the expertise of freelancers or agencies to streamline your operations and scale your affiliate marketing business efficiently.

Investing in your affiliate marketing business is crucial for long-term growth and success. Here are some key areas to consider when making investments:

1. Education and Training: Invest in your knowledge and skills by attending courses, workshops, or conferences related to affiliate marketing. Stay updated with industry trends, marketing strategies, and new technologies. Continuous learning will enhance your expertise and give you a competitive edge.

2. Quality Content Creation: Invest in creating high-quality content that provides value to your audience. Hire professional writers, photographers, or videographers if needed. Engaging content can attract more visitors, increase conversions, and improve your overall credibility.

3. Website Optimization: Invest in optimizing your website for a better user experience and higher search engine rankings. Improve site speed, design, mobile responsiveness, and navigation. Consider hiring a web developer or investing in website optimization tools to enhance performance.

4. SEO and Digital Marketing Tools: Invest in SEO tools, keyword research software, and digital marketing automation tools. These tools can help you optimize your content, track rankings, analyze data, and automate marketing campaigns, saving you time and improving efficiency.

5. Paid Advertising Campaigns: Consider investing in paid advertising campaigns to drive targeted traffic to your website. Platforms like Google Ads, Facebook Ads, or influencer collaborations can expand your reach and attract new customers. Set a budget and monitor the performance of your campaigns closely.

6. Affiliate Marketing Tools and Platforms: Invest in affiliate marketing tools and platforms to streamline your operations and track your performance effectively. These tools can help you manage affiliate links, analyze data, monitor conversions, and optimize your campaigns.

7. Email Marketing Automation: Invest in email marketing software to build and nurture your email list. Implement automation to send personalized emails, track open rates, and automate follow-ups. Email marketing can be a powerful tool for generating affiliate sales and building relationships with your audience.

8. Professional Networking and Collaboration: Invest time and effort in building professional relationships within the affiliate marketing industry. Attend industry events, join online communities, and connect with other affiliates, merchants, and influencers. Collaboration and networking can lead to new opportunities and mutual growth. Remember, investments in your affiliate business should be strategic and aligned with your goals. Regularly evaluate the return on investment (ROI) of your investments and adjust your strategies accordingly. By investing wisely, you can accelerate the growth of your affiliate marketing business and maximize your long-term profitability.

Expanding into new niches or markets can help diversify your income streams and grow your affiliate marketing business. Here's how to effectively explore new niches or markets:

1. Research and Analysis: Conduct thorough market research to identify potential niches or markets that align with your expertise, interests, and audience. Analyze competition, demand, profitability, and trends to assess the viability of expanding into a new niche.

2. Understand the Target Audience: Understand the needs, preferences, and pain points of the target audience in the new niche or market. Adapt your content, promotional strategies, and product recommendations to cater to their specific needs effectively.

3. Content Strategy and SEO: Develop a content strategy tailored to the new niche. Create valuable and targeted content that addresses the unique interests and concerns of the audience. Optimize your content for relevant keywords and implement SEO strategies to increase visibility in search results.

4. Partner with New Merchants: Identify affiliate programs or merchants that offer products or services related to the new niche. Research their reputation, commission structures, and affiliate support. Build relationships with these merchants and leverage their resources to promote relevant products to your audience.

5. Adjust Marketing Channels: Explore new marketing channels or platforms that are popular in the new niche or market. This may include social media platforms, forums, online communities, or industry-specific websites. Adapt your marketing efforts to effectively reach and engage with the target audience in the new niche.

6. Monitor Performance and Adapt: Regularly monitor the performance of your expansion efforts. Assess the engagement, conversions, and revenue generated from the new niche or market. Analyze the data, identify areas for improvement, and make necessary adjustments to optimize your strategies.

In addition to affiliate marketing, there are various other monetization strategies you can consider to diversify your income. Here are a few options:

1. Sponsored Content: Collaborate with brands for sponsored content opportunities. Create engaging content that promotes their products or services and disclose any sponsorships to maintain transparency.

2. Digital Products or Courses: Develop and sell your own digital products, such as e-books, online courses, templates, or software tools. Leverage your expertise to provide value and monetize your knowledge.

3. Display Advertising: Utilize display advertising networks like Google AdSense or Media.net to place targeted ads on your

---

website. Optimize ad placements to balance user experience and revenue generation.

4. Membership or Subscription Model: Create premium content or offer exclusive perks through a membership or subscription model. Provide additional value to subscribers and generate recurring revenue.

5. Brand Partnerships or Influencer Marketing: Leverage your influence and audience to partner with brands as an influencer. Collaborate on sponsored campaigns, brand ambassadorships, or product endorsements.

6. Online Courses or Coaching Services: Share your expertise by offering online courses or coaching services related to your niche. Provide personalized guidance and support to learners or clients.

Evaluate these monetization strategies based on their suitability to your audience, niche, and expertise. Consider testing different strategies, tracking their performance, and adjusting your approach accordingly. Diversifying your income streams can help stabilize your business and unlock new revenue opportunities.

15.1 COMMON PITFALLS FOR BEGINNERS

As a beginner in affiliate marketing, it's important to be aware of common pitfalls to avoid unnecessary setbacks. Here are some mistakes to steer clear of:

1. Choosing the Wrong Niche: Selecting the wrong niche can hinder your success. Choose a niche that aligns with your interests, knowledge, and has a profitable market. Research the demand, competition, and potential for growth before committing to a niche.

2. Promoting Irrelevant Products: Promoting products or services that are irrelevant to your audience can lead to low engagement and poor conversions. Focus on products that genuinely solve your audience's problems or meet their needs. Stay true to your niche and provide value through relevant recommendations.

3. Neglecting Audience Building: Building an engaged audience is crucial for affiliate marketing success. Don't solely focus on promoting products. Invest time and effort in cultivating a loyal following by creating valuable content, engaging with your audience, and building trust. Neglecting audience building can limit your long-term growth potential.

4. Not Disclosing Affiliate Relationships: Failing to disclose your affiliate relationships can erode trust with your audience and potentially violate FTC guidelines. Always disclose your affiliate relationships clearly and conspicuously. Be transparent about your financial interests and maintain the integrity of your recommendations.

5. Relying Solely on One Affiliate Program: Depending on a single affiliate program for all your earnings can be risky. Diversify your income sources by partnering with multiple reputable affiliate programs. This reduces the impact of

program changes, commission rate fluctuations, or potential program terminations.

6. Ignoring SEO and Traffic Generation: Neglecting search engine optimization (SEO) and traffic generation can limit your visibility and hinder your affiliate marketing success. Understand SEO basics, optimize your content for relevant keywords, and employ strategies to drive targeted traffic to your website or platform.

7. Not Tracking and Analyzing Performance: Failing to track and analyze your performance metrics can prevent you from identifying what works and what needs improvement. Utilize analytics tools to monitor key performance indicators (KPIs) such as traffic, conversions, click-through rates, and earnings. This data helps you make informed decisions and optimize your strategies.

8. Overlooking Continuous Learning: Affiliate marketing is a dynamic field, and staying updated with industry trends, strategies, and technologies is essential. Commit to continuous

learning through courses, forums, industry blogs, and networking events. This helps you adapt to changes, refine your skills, and remain competitive. Avoiding these common pitfalls can set you on the path to affiliate marketing success.

Learn from others' experiences, adapt your strategies, and remain focused on providing value to your audience. With dedication, continuous learning, and avoiding these mistakes, you can increase your chances of building a thriving affiliate marketing business.

15.2 AVOIDING SCAMS AND SHADY PROGRAMS

When engaging in affiliate marketing, it's crucial to protect yourself from scams and shady programs that can harm your reputation and financial well-being. Here are some tips to avoid falling victim to fraudulent schemes:

1. Research Affiliate Programs and Merchants:

Thoroughly research affiliate programs and merchants before partnering with them. Look for established, reputable companies with positive reviews and a solid track record. Verify their legitimacy, financial stability, and customer satisfaction levels.

2. Beware of High-Payout Promises: Be cautious of programs promising unusually high commission rates or payouts. If an offer sounds too good to be true, it likely is. Research industry standards to understand typical commission rates for your niche.

3. Check for Transparency and Clear Policies: Legitimate affiliate programs provide clear terms and conditions, commission structures, and payout schedules. Avoid programs that lack transparency or have ambiguous policies. Read program agreements thoroughly and clarify any doubts before joining.

4. Assess Merchant Reputation: Evaluate the reputation and credibility of the merchants you promote. Conduct online research, check customer reviews, and assess their customer

service. Promoting reputable brands helps maintain your own credibility and protects your audience.

5. Avoid Pyramid or Multi-Level Marketing Schemes:

Be cautious of programs that resemble pyramid or multi-level marketing (MLM) schemes. These often prioritize recruitment over product quality and sustainability. Focus on promoting products or services that provide genuine value to customers.

6. Be Wary of Excessive Upfront Costs: Avoid programs

that require significant upfront fees or investments. Legitimate affiliate programs typically do not require substantial financial commitments upfront. Be cautious of programs that promise success only after significant monetary investment.

7. Verify Affiliate Program Terms and Conditions:

Thoroughly review the terms and conditions of affiliate programs before joining. Pay attention to payout thresholds, payment methods, cookie duration, and any exclusivity clauses.

Ensure the program aligns with your business goals and requirements.

8. Trust Your Instincts and Seek Advice: If something feels off or suspicious, trust your instincts. Seek advice from trusted industry experts or affiliate marketing communities. Engage in discussions and ask for feedback before making any decisions. By exercising caution, conducting thorough research, and trusting your instincts, you can avoid scams and protect yourself from fraudulent affiliate programs. Prioritize working with reputable merchants and programs that offer transparency, fair commissions, and long-term sustainability. Safeguarding your reputation and financial well-being is essential for a successful and ethical affiliate marketing journey.

15.3 BALANCING PROMOTIONAL AND NON-PROMOTIONAL CONTENT

Finding the right balance between promotional and non-promotional content is crucial in maintaining a healthy relationship with your audience.

Here are some tips to strike the right balance:

1. Provide Value with Non-Promotional Content:
Create non-promotional content that is valuable, informative, and entertaining for your audience. This can include educational articles, how-to guides, industry insights, or entertaining stories. Aim to establish yourself as a trusted source of information in your niche.

2. Understand Your Audience's Needs: Get to know your audience and understand their needs, interests, and pain points. Tailor your non-promotional content to address these aspects and offer solutions or valuable insights. By consistently delivering relevant content, you build trust and maintain engagement.

3. Use a Soft-Sell Approach: Instead of solely focusing on selling, adopt a soft-sell approach in your promotional content. Educate your audience about the benefits and value of the products or services you recommend. Explain how they can address specific pain points or enhance their lives.

4. Contextualize Promotions within Non-Promotional Content: Integrate your promotional content within your non-promotional content in a seamless and contextual manner. For example, include product recommendations or affiliate links in relevant product reviews, tutorials, or recommended resource lists. This way, promotions feel natural and useful to your audience.

5. Be Transparent and Disclose Affiliate Relationships: Maintain transparency with your audience by clearly disclosing your affiliate relationships. This builds trust and ensures that your audience understands the nature of your recommendations. Disclose affiliate links within your content or use disclaimer statements to maintain transparency.

6. Focus on Quality over Quantity: Prioritize quality over quantity when it comes to promotional content. Select products or services that align with your audience's interests and needs.

Promote only those that you genuinely believe in and have thoroughly evaluated for their value.

7. Monitor Engagement and Feedback: Monitor the engagement and feedback from your audience regarding your promotional and non-promotional content. Pay attention to their responses, comments, and engagement metrics. Adjust your approach based on the feedback received to strike the right balance.

8. Test and Evaluate Performance: Experiment with different content formats, topics, and promotional strategies. Track the performance of your content using analytics tools to determine what resonates best with your audience. This helps you refine your content strategy and strike a balance that works for your specific audience. By striking the right balance between promotional and non-promotional content, you keep your audience engaged, maintain their trust, and ensure a positive user experience. Providing value through non-promotional

content establishes your authority and credibility, making your promotional content more effective and meaningful.

15.4 NEGLECTING SEO AND USER EXPERIENCE

Neglecting search engine optimization (SEO) and user experience can hinder the success of your affiliate marketing efforts.

Here are some common mistakes to avoid:

1. **Ignoring Keyword Research:** Keyword research is essential for optimizing your content to rank well in search engine results. Neglecting keyword research means missing out on valuable organic traffic. Identify relevant keywords and incorporate them strategically in your content to improve visibility and attract targeted visitors.

2. **Over-Optimizing or Keyword Stuffing:** While keyword optimization is important, over-optimizing or keyword stuffing can negatively impact user experience and search engine rankings. Aim for a natural and seamless integration of

keywords within your content, ensuring it reads well and provides value to the reader.

3. Poor Website Structure and Navigation: A poorly structured website with confusing navigation can frustrate visitors and lead to high bounce rates. Optimize your website's structure and navigation to make it user-friendly. Organize your content logically, create clear categories, and ensure easy access to important pages.

4. Slow Page Load Speed: Slow-loading pages can negatively affect user experience and search engine rankings. Optimize your website's speed by minimizing file sizes, optimizing images, leveraging caching techniques, and using a reliable hosting provider.

5. Lack of Mobile Responsiveness: With the increasing use of mobile devices, neglecting mobile responsiveness can result in a poor user experience. Ensure your website is mobile-friendly and responsive across different screen sizes. Test your

website on various devices to ensure a seamless experience for mobile users.

6. Inadequate Content Formatting: Presenting content in a cluttered or unformatted manner can deter users from engaging with it. Use headings, subheadings, bullet points, and other formatting techniques to make your content scannable and easy to read. Incorporate visual elements like images or infographics to enhance user experience.

7. Poor Internal and External Linking: Neglecting internal and external linking can impact SEO and user experience. Use internal links to guide users to relevant content within your website, improving navigation and encouraging deeper engagement. External links to reputable sources can add credibility and value to your content.

8. Lack of User-Friendly Design: A visually unappealing or cluttered design can turn off users and affect engagement. Prioritize a clean, user-friendly design with clear typography, readable fonts, and an intuitive layout. Make sure your website

is visually appealing, aligns with your brand, and enhances the overall user experience. By prioritizing SEO and user experience, you can improve your website's visibility, attract more targeted traffic, and provide a positive experience for your audience. Continuously monitor your website's performance, track user behavior, and optimize your strategies to align with search engine guidelines and user preferences. Striking the right balance between SEO optimization and user experience will enhance your affiliate marketing success.

16.1 ANALYZING SUCCESSFUL AFFILIATE WEBSITES

Studying successful affiliate websites can provide valuable insights into effective strategies and tactics. Here are some key aspects to analyze when studying successful affiliate websites:

1. Niche Selection: Identify the niche the website operates in. Analyze how the chosen niche aligns with the target audience's interests and needs. Consider the potential for profitability and competition within the niche.

2. Content Strategy: Examine the website's content strategy. Look at the types of content they create, such as product reviews, tutorials, comparison articles, or informative blog posts. Assess how the content addresses the target audience's pain points and provides value.

3. SEO Optimization: Evaluate the website's search engine optimization (SEO) efforts. Consider factors such as keyword

research, on-page optimization, backlink profile, and overall site structure. Analyze how effectively the website ranks in search engine results pages (SERPs) for relevant keywords.

4. User Experience: Assess the website's user experience. Look at factors such as site speed, mobile responsiveness, intuitive navigation, and visual appeal. Analyze how the website engages and retains visitors, encourages interaction, and provides a positive user experience.

5. Monetization Strategies: Examine the website's monetization strategies. Identify the affiliate programs or partnerships they have established. Evaluate how effectively they integrate affiliate links into their content and whether they offer additional revenue streams, such as sponsored content or digital products.

6. Audience Engagement: Analyze how the website engages with its audience. Look at the website's interaction on social media platforms, the presence of a mailing list, or the use of

comment sections. Assess the level of audience engagement, community building, and the strategies employed to foster user interaction.

7. Conversion Optimization: Evaluate how the website optimizes conversions. Consider the placement and design of call-to-action buttons, the use of persuasive copywriting, and the strategies employed to encourage click-throughs and conversions. Assess whether they employ effective conversion tracking and testing techniques.

8. Branding and Authority: Examine how the website establishes its brand and authority. Look at the website's overall design, branding elements, tone of voice, and consistency across various channels. Analyze how the website positions itself as a trusted resource and builds authority within its niche.

Understand the specific techniques they use to attract and engage their audience, optimize conversions, and monetize their efforts effectively. However, keep in mind that each case study is unique, and it's essential to adapt these insights to fit your own niche, audience, and business goals.

Interviews with successful affiliate marketers can provide valuable firsthand insights into their strategies, experiences, and lessons learned. Here are some key areas to explore during interviews with successful affiliate marketers:

1. **Background and Journey:** Gain an understanding of the affiliate marketer's background, including how they got started in affiliate marketing and their journey to success. Ask about their motivations, challenges faced, and pivotal moments that shaped their affiliate marketing career.

2. **Niche Selection and Audience Targeting:** Discuss how the affiliate marketer selected their niche and identified their target audience. Explore the process they went through to understand their audience's needs, interests, and pain points.

Learn how they positioned themselves as an authority within their niche.

3. **Content Strategy and Creation:** Inquire about the affiliate marketer's content strategy. Explore the types of content they create, how they approach content planning, and their process for content creation. Learn how they ensure their content provides value, resonates with their audience, and drives conversions.

4. **SEO and Traffic Generation:** Discuss the affiliate marketer's approach to search engine optimization (SEO) and traffic generation. Explore the strategies they employ to drive organic traffic, the importance of keyword research, and their tactics for improving search engine rankings. Inquire about any other traffic generation methods they utilize, such as social media or paid advertising.

5. **Affiliate Partnerships and Monetization:** Explore the affiliate marketer's approach to forming partnerships with merchants and selecting affiliate programs. Inquire about their

criteria for choosing affiliate programs, their strategies for promoting affiliate products, and how they ensure a seamless integration of affiliate links into their content. Discuss other monetization strategies they employ, such as sponsored content or digital products.

6. Building and Engaging with an Audience: Ask about the affiliate marketer's strategies for building and engaging with their audience. Inquire about their approach to social media, email marketing, or community building. Learn how they foster relationships with their audience, encourage interaction, and maintain ongoing engagement.

7. Overcoming Challenges and Lessons Learned: Discuss the challenges the affiliate marketer faced along their journey and how they overcame them. Inquire about any mistakes made and the lessons learned from those experiences. Learn about the strategies they employ to stay updated with

industry trends and continually improve their affiliate marketing efforts.

8. Advice for Beginners: Ask the successful affiliate marketer for their advice to beginners entering the field. Inquire about the key tips, strategies, or mindsets they believe are important for success in affiliate marketing. Encourage them to share any resources, tools, or communities they found helpful during their journey. By learning from their experiences, strategies, and lessons learned, you can gain valuable knowledge and apply it to your own affiliate marketing endeavors.

16.3 LESSONS LEARNED FROM SUCCESS STORIES

Success stories of affiliate marketers can provide valuable lessons and inspiration for those seeking to achieve their own success in the field.

Here are some key lessons that can be learned from these success stories:

1. **Persistence and Dedication:** Successful affiliate marketers emphasize the importance of persistence and dedication. Building a successful affiliate marketing business takes time and effort. It requires consistent content creation, audience engagement, and staying updated with industry trends. Don't get discouraged by initial challenges or slow progress. Stay committed and keep pushing forward.

2. **Understanding the Target Audience:** One common theme among successful affiliate marketers is a deep understanding of their target audience. They invest time in researching their audience's needs, preferences, and pain points. By understanding their audience, they can create relevant and valuable content that resonates with their readers and drives conversions.

3. **Providing Value and Building Trust:** Successful affiliates prioritize providing value to their audience. They focus on creating high-quality content that educates, informs, and

solves problems. By consistently delivering value, they build trust with their audience, positioning themselves as credible sources of information and recommendations.

4. Diversifying Income Streams: Successful affiliates understand the importance of diversifying their income streams. They explore various monetization strategies, such as affiliate programs, sponsored content, digital products, or consulting services. This diversification helps mitigate risks and provides multiple revenue streams to sustain and grow their businesses.

5. Continuous Learning and Adaptation: Affiliate marketing is an ever-evolving field, and successful affiliates emphasize the importance of continuous learning. They stay updated with industry trends, algorithm changes, and marketing strategies. They experiment, test, and adapt their approaches based on the results and feedback they receive.

6. Building Relationships and Networking: Networking and building relationships within the affiliate marketing

community can be instrumental in achieving success. Successful affiliates engage in collaborations, joint ventures, and partnerships with other affiliates, merchants, or industry influencers. These connections can open doors to new opportunities, expand their reach, and provide valuable insights and support.

7. Tracking and Analyzing Performance: Successful affiliates pay close attention to their performance metrics. They track data, analyze conversions, click-through rates, and other key performance indicators. By understanding their data, they can identify what strategies and tactics are working and make informed decisions to optimize their efforts.

8. Authenticity and Transparency: Authenticity and transparency are essential for long-term success. Successful affiliates prioritize being genuine and transparent with their audience. They disclose their affiliate relationships, clearly communicate their motivations, and only promote products or

services they truly believe in. This builds trust and credibility with their audience. Remember that success is a result of consistent effort, understanding your audience, providing value, and adapting to the ever-changing landscape of affiliate marketing. Learn from success stories, but also forge your own unique path based on your strengths, interests, and the needs of your audience.

16.4 APPLYING CASE STUDY INSIGHTS TO YOUR BUSINESS

When studying case studies of successful affiliate marketers, it's important to apply the insights gained to your own business. Here are some steps to effectively apply case study insights:

1. Identify Relevant Insights: Identify the specific insights from the case studies that resonate with your business goals and target audience. Focus on the strategies, tactics, or approaches that align with your niche and resonate with your audience's needs.

2. Adapt to Your Unique Situation: Remember that each case study is unique, and what worked for one affiliate marketer may not work exactly the same way for you. Adapt the insights to fit your own business, audience, and available resources. Consider how you can incorporate the ideas into your existing strategy.

3. Set Clear Goals: Define clear goals for your affiliate marketing business. Consider your long-term vision, revenue targets, audience engagement goals, and content objectives. The case study insights should support these goals and help you achieve them more effectively.

4. Develop an Action Plan: Based on the insights, develop an action plan that outlines the steps you need to take to implement the strategies and tactics. Break down the plan into actionable tasks with timelines and milestones to keep yourself accountable.

5. Experiment and Measure Results: Implement the strategies from the case studies in your business and track the results. Set up metrics and key performance indicators (KPIs) to monitor the effectiveness of the implemented strategies. Analyze the data to understand what works and what needs adjustments.

6. Iterate and Improve: Based on the results and feedback you gather, iterate and improve your strategies. Be open to making changes and refining your approach to better align with your audience's preferences and the evolving industry landscape. Continuously learn, adapt, and optimize your efforts.

7. Seek Feedback and Support: Seek feedback from your audience, peers, or mentors. Join affiliate marketing communities or engage with industry experts to gain insights and support. Collaborate with others to share experiences and learn from each other's successes and challenges.

8. Stay Updated and Evolve: Stay updated with industry trends, algorithm changes, and emerging strategies. Continuously educate yourself through industry blogs, podcasts, courses, or conferences. Embrace a growth mindset

and be willing to evolve your strategies as the affiliate marketing landscape evolves. By applying case study insights to your own business, you can benefit from the experiences and strategies of successful affiliate marketers. However, always remember to adapt and customize these insights to fit your unique circumstances and audience. Use them as inspiration and guidance to shape your own path toward success in affiliate marketing.

17.1 TRENDS IMPACTING THE AFFILIATE MARKETING INDUSTRY

The affiliate marketing industry continues to evolve and adapt to changing consumer behaviors, technology advancements, and industry trends. Here are some key trends that are impacting the future of affiliate marketing:

1. Influencer Marketing: Influencer marketing is on the rise and has become a significant part of the affiliate marketing landscape. Brands are increasingly partnering with influencers who have large and engaged audiences to promote their products or services. Influencer marketing brings a more personalized and authentic approach to affiliate marketing, as influencers leverage their authority and trust with their followers.

2. Mobile and App-Based Affiliate Marketing: With the increasing use of mobile devices, mobile and app-based affiliate marketing is gaining momentum.

Affiliates are optimizing their websites and content for mobile users and exploring opportunities to promote affiliate products through mobile apps. This trend reflects the growing importance of providing a seamless user experience on mobile devices.

3. Voice Search and Smart Speakers: The rise of voice search technology and smart speakers is shaping the way people search for information and make purchasing decisions. Affiliate marketers are adapting their content and SEO strategies to optimize for voice search queries. Voice commerce, where users make purchases through voice commands, presents new opportunities for affiliate marketers to reach and engage with their audience.

4. Artificial Intelligence (AI) and Machine Learning (ML): AI and ML technologies are revolutionizing the affiliate marketing industry. These technologies enable affiliates to gather and analyze large amounts of data, personalize content, and deliver more targeted recommendations. AI-powered chatbots and virtual assistants are also being used to enhance customer support and engagement in the affiliate marketing space.

5. Video Content and Live Streaming: Video content, including product reviews, tutorials, and live streaming, is becoming increasingly popular among consumers. Affiliates are leveraging video platforms like YouTube, TikTok, and live streaming platforms to promote affiliate products and engage with their audience in more interactive ways. Video content offers a more immersive and engaging experience, helping affiliates build trust and influence purchasing decisions.

6. Sustainable and Ethical Affiliate Marketing: Consumers are becoming more conscious of sustainability and ethical practices. Affiliate marketers are aligning with brands that share these values, promoting sustainable and ethical products or services. Affiliates are transparently communicating their affiliations and supporting causes that resonate with their audience, fostering trust and loyalty.

7. Cross-Channel Marketing and Attribution: Cross-channel marketing and attribution are gaining importance in affiliate marketing. Affiliates are leveraging multiple marketing channels, such as social media, email, content marketing, and paid advertising, to reach and engage with their audience.

Attribution models are being refined to give proper credit to the touchpoints that contribute to conversions, allowing affiliates to better track and optimize their marketing efforts.

8. Data Privacy and Compliance: With the increasing focus on data privacy and regulations like the General Data Protection Regulation (GDPR) and the California Consumer Privacy Act (CCPA), affiliates are prioritizing data privacy and compliance. They are transparently disclosing their data collection practices and ensuring compliance with privacy regulations to build trust with their audience.

These trends shape the future of affiliate marketing, and staying ahead of them is crucial for success. Affiliate marketers need to adapt their strategies, embrace emerging technologies, and align with changing consumer behaviors to remain competitive in the evolving affiliate marketing landscape. By keeping a pulse on these trends, affiliates can position themselves for growth and capitalize on new opportunities.

17.2 TECHNOLOGICAL INNOVATIONS AFFECTING AFFILIATE MARKETING

Technological innovations play a significant role in shaping the future of affiliate marketing. Here are some key technological advancements that are impacting the affiliate marketing industry:

1. Artificial Intelligence (AI) and Machine Learning (ML): AI and ML technologies are revolutionizing affiliate marketing by automating processes, personalizing recommendations, and optimizing marketing strategies. AI-powered algorithms can analyze vast amounts of data to identify trends, understand consumer behavior, and improve targeting. ML helps affiliates deliver more relevant content and recommendations to their audience, enhancing user experiences and boosting conversions.

2. Big Data and Advanced Analytics: The availability of big data and advanced analytics tools enables affiliate marketers to gain deep insights into consumer behavior, preferences, and purchasing patterns. Affiliates can leverage data analytics to refine their targeting, track performance, and make data-driven decisions. The ability to extract actionable insights from data empowers affiliates to optimize their campaigns and improve overall performance.

3. Voice Search and Smart Assistants: The increasing adoption of voice search technology and smart assistants like Amazon Alexa and Google Assistant has implications for affiliate marketing. Affiliates need to optimize their content for voice search queries to ensure visibility in voice search results. Voice commerce, where users make purchases through voice commands, presents new opportunities for affiliates to integrate their recommendations into voice-enabled shopping experiences.

4. Augmented Reality (AR) and Virtual Reality (VR): AR and VR technologies are transforming the way consumers interact with products and make purchase decisions. Affiliates can leverage AR and VR to provide immersive and interactive experiences for their audience. For example, showcasing products through AR try-on experiences or virtual tours can enhance engagement and increase conversions.

5. Blockchain Technology: Blockchain technology has the potential to address issues of transparency and trust in affiliate marketing. By leveraging blockchain, affiliates can track transactions securely, ensure fair commission attribution, and increase trust between affiliates, merchants, and consumers. Blockchain-based affiliate networks and smart contracts have the potential to streamline transactions and eliminate fraudulent activities.

6. Chatbots and Conversational AI: Chatbots and conversational AI are transforming customer support and engagement in affiliate marketing. Affiliates can use chatbots to provide instant assistance, answer queries, and guide users through their purchasing journey. Conversational AI allows for personalized and interactive conversations, enhancing user experiences and increasing engagement.

7. Mobile Technology and Apps: The ubiquity of mobile devices and the popularity of mobile apps have a profound impact on affiliate marketing. Affiliates need to optimize their websites and content for mobile users, ensuring responsive design, fast load times, and seamless user experiences.

Mobile apps provide affiliates with new channels to reach and engage their audience, leveraging push notifications and app-specific features.

8. Social Media and Influencer Platforms: Social media platforms and influencer marketing continue to shape the affiliate marketing landscape. Affiliates can leverage social media to reach a wider audience, engage with followers, and promote affiliate products. Influencer platforms facilitate collaborations between affiliates and influencers, enabling targeted promotional campaigns and authentic product recommendations.

Keeping up with technological innovations is essential for affiliate marketers to stay relevant and thrive in the industry. By embracing emerging technologies, affiliates can enhance their marketing strategies, improve user experiences, and capitalize on new opportunities that arise from technological advancements.

17.3 PREDICTIONS FOR AFFILIATE MARKETING IN THE NEXT DECADE

Looking ahead, here are some predictions for the future of affiliate marketing in the next decade:

1. Continued Growth of Influencer Marketing: Influencer marketing will continue to grow in importance as influencers establish themselves as trusted authorities in their respective niches. Brands will increasingly leverage the influence and reach of influencers to promote their products and drive affiliate sales. Influencer marketing will become an integral part of affiliate marketing strategies.

2. Rise of Micro-Influencers: Micro-influencers, individuals with smaller but highly engaged social media followings, will gain prominence in affiliate marketing. Brands will recognize the value of targeted and niche audiences that micro-influencers can reach. Collaborations with micro-influencers will allow affiliates to tap into highly engaged and loyal communities for better conversion rates.

3. Expansion of Video and Live Streaming: Video content and live streaming will continue to dominate the digital landscape. Affiliates will increasingly rely on platforms like YouTube, TikTok, Instagram Live, and Twitch to create engaging video content that drives affiliate sales. Video reviews, tutorials, and product demonstrations will become even more influential in shaping consumer purchase decisions.

4. Integration of Artificial Intelligence (AI) and Automation: AI and automation technologies will become more prevalent in affiliate marketing. Affiliates will leverage AI-powered tools for data analysis, content personalization, and audience targeting. Automation will streamline repetitive tasks, allowing affiliates to focus more on strategy, content creation, and building relationships with their audience and partners.

5. Enhanced Personalization and User Experience: Affiliates will prioritize personalization and user experience to stand out in a competitive landscape. They will utilize data-driven insights to deliver highly targeted content and recommendations to their audience. Websites and content will be optimized for a seamless user experience across devices, ensuring faster load times, intuitive navigation, and interactive elements.

6. Shift Towards Ethical and Sustainable Marketing: Consumers' increasing emphasis on ethical and sustainable practices will drive affiliates to align with brands that share these values. Affiliates will promote products and services that are environmentally friendly, socially responsible, and align with their audience's values. Transparency and authenticity in marketing efforts will be key to gaining consumer trust.

7. Expansion of Cross-Border Affiliate Marketing: Affiliate marketing will see a significant expansion into global markets. Affiliates will collaborate with international brands, targeting audiences across different regions and cultures. As technology enables easier cross-border transactions and communication, affiliates will tap into new markets, diversify their revenue streams, and reach a wider global audience.

8. Focus on Data Privacy and Security: As data privacy regulations evolve, affiliates will prioritize compliance and safeguarding user data. They will ensure transparent data collection practices, secure transaction processes, and build trust with their audience by emphasizing data privacy and security measures.

Protecting user data will be paramount to maintain a positive reputation and foster long-term relationships. These predictions highlight the ongoing evolution of affiliate marketing, driven by changing consumer behavior, technological advancements, and industry trends. Affiliate marketers who adapt to these shifts, embrace emerging technologies, and prioritize user experience and authenticity will be well-positioned for success in the next decade.

17.4 ADAPTING TO CHANGE IN THE AFFILIATE INDUSTRY

The affiliate marketing industry is constantly evolving, and staying adaptable is crucial for long-term success. Here are some strategies to effectively adapt to change in the affiliate industry:

1. Stay Informed and Embrace New Technologies: Keep a pulse on industry news, trends, and emerging technologies. Stay informed about changes in algorithms, new marketing channels, and technological advancements.

Embrace new technologies that can enhance your marketing efforts, such as AI, automation tools, or data analytics platforms.

2. Continuously Learn and Upskill: Invest in your knowledge and skills to stay ahead of the curve. Attend industry conferences, webinars, and workshops to learn from experts and expand your understanding of affiliate marketing. Stay up to date with best practices, new strategies, and marketing techniques through online resources, courses, or mentorship programs.

3. Adapt Your Content Strategy: Monitor changes in consumer behavior and adjust your content strategy accordingly. Consider new content formats, such as video, podcasts, or interactive content, that align with evolving audience preferences. Experiment with different content distribution channels, including social media platforms or emerging niche communities.

4. Diversify Your Traffic Sources: Relying solely on one traffic source can be risky.

Explore and diversify your traffic sources to mitigate potential disruptions caused by algorithm changes or shifts in consumer behavior. Explore paid advertising, social media marketing, influencer collaborations, SEO optimization, email marketing, or partnerships with other affiliates.

5. Foster Relationships and Collaboration: Build relationships with other affiliates, merchants, influencers, and industry experts. Collaboration can lead to new opportunities, shared insights, and cross-promotion. Engage in networking events, affiliate communities, and online forums to connect with like-minded professionals and stay connected with the latest industry developments.

6. Prioritize User Experience and Personalization: User experience and personalization are paramount in affiliate marketing. Adapt your strategies to provide seamless and relevant experiences for your audience. Leverage technologies like AI and automation to personalize content, recommendations, and user journeys. Continuously optimize your website, mobile experience, and conversion funnels to enhance user satisfaction.

7. Monitor and Analyze Performance: Regularly monitor and analyze your performance metrics to identify areas for improvement and adapt your strategies accordingly. Use tracking tools, analytics platforms, and conversion tracking to gain insights into your audience's behavior, conversion rates, and engagement levels. Make data-driven decisions to optimize your campaigns and maximize your results.

8. Adapt to Regulatory Changes: Stay up to date with regulatory changes and comply with legal obligations, such as data privacy regulations and disclosure requirements. Adapt your practices to ensure transparency, trust, and compliance. Regularly review your privacy policies, cookie consent mechanisms, and disclosure statements to maintain a strong ethical foundation.

Adapting to change requires a proactive and agile mindset. Embrace new technologies, invest in continuous learning, and be open to experimenting with new strategies. Stay connected with industry peers, monitor performance data, and prioritize user experience to stay ahead in the dynamic landscape of the affiliate industry.

18.1 CREATING YOUR AFFILIATE MARKETING PLAN

Creating a well-defined affiliate marketing plan is crucial for a successful start in the industry. Here are the key steps to develop your affiliate marketing plan for your first 90 days:

1. Set Clear Goals: Define your goals for the first 90 days in affiliate marketing. Consider what you want to achieve in terms of revenue, audience growth, content creation, or partnerships. Set specific, measurable, attainable, relevant, and time-bound (SMART) goals to guide your efforts.

2. Identify Your Target Audience: Research and identify your target audience. Understand their demographics, interests, pain points, and online behavior. Determine how your chosen niche aligns with your target audience's needs and preferences. This knowledge will guide your content creation and marketing strategies.

3. Select Your Niche: Choose a niche that you are passionate about and has potential for profitability. Consider your interests, expertise, and the market demand for the niche. Ensure that your chosen niche aligns with your target audience's interests and provides opportunities for promoting affiliate products.

4. Research Affiliate Programs: Identify and research affiliate programs within your chosen niche. Look for reputable programs that offer products or services that resonate with your audience. Consider factors such as commission rates, cookie durations, payout methods, and affiliate support. Choose programs that align with your goals and audience preferences.

5. Develop Your Content Strategy: Craft a content strategy that caters to your target audience's needs and preferences. Determine the types of content you will create, such as product reviews, tutorials, comparison articles, or informative blog posts. Plan a content calendar, outlining topics, keywords, and publication dates to ensure consistent content creation.

6. Build Your Online Platform: Set up your online platform, which may include a website, blog, or social media channels. Create a user-friendly website design, optimize it for search engines, and ensure mobile responsiveness. Incorporate affiliate links strategically into your content and design. Implement analytics and tracking tools to monitor your website's performance.

7. Promote Your Content and Build an Audience: Develop a promotion strategy to drive traffic to your content and build an audience. Utilize social media platforms, guest blogging, forums, or influencer collaborations to expand your reach. Engage with your audience through comments, email newsletters, or social media interactions to foster a loyal following.

8. Track Performance and Optimize: Regularly track and analyze your performance metrics to measure the effectiveness of your efforts. Monitor key performance indicators (KPIs) such as traffic, conversion rates, click-through rates, and revenue. Use the insights gained to optimize your content, marketing strategies, and affiliate partnerships.

9. Cultivate Relationships and Partnerships: Build relationships with other affiliates, influencers, and merchants within your niche. Collaborate on joint ventures, guest posting, or cross-promotion opportunities to expand your network and reach. Leverage partnerships to tap into new audiences and gain valuable insights and support from industry peers.

10. Stay Educated and Adapt: Stay updated with industry trends, changes in algorithms, and new marketing strategies. Continuously educate yourself through industry resources, courses, and webinars. Adapt your strategies based on feedback, market trends, and data analysis to enhance your performance and stay ahead of the competition.

By creating a well-thought-out affiliate marketing plan, you can lay a solid foundation for your first 90 days in the industry. Define your goals, understand your target audience, develop a content strategy, and build your online platform. Stay focused, track your performance, adapt to feedback, and continue to learn and grow throughout the process.

18.2 SETTING UP YOUR AFFILIATE MARKETING ASSETS

To kickstart your affiliate marketing journey, it's crucial to set up your affiliate marketing assets. Here are the key components to focus on when setting up your affiliate marketing assets:

1. **Website or Blog:** Set up a professional website or blog as your central hub for affiliate marketing activities. Choose a domain name that reflects your niche and is easy to remember. Select a reliable web hosting service and install a user-friendly content management system (CMS) like WordPress. Customize your website's design, layout, and branding to create a visually appealing and cohesive online presence.

2. **Content Strategy:** Develop a content strategy that aligns with your niche and target audience. Determine the types of content you will create, such as product reviews, tutorials, guides, or informative articles. Plan your content calendar with a consistent publishing schedule to keep your audience engaged. Ensure that your content provides value, solves problems, and offers relevant affiliate product recommendations.

3. **Landing Pages:** Create dedicated landing pages that highlight specific affiliate products or promotions. Optimize these pages to drive conversions by including persuasive copy, compelling call-to-action buttons, and visually appealing elements. Implement tracking codes and analytics to measure the performance of your landing pages and make data-driven optimizations.

4. **Email Marketing:** Set up an email marketing system to build and nurture your subscriber list. Offer valuable lead magnets, such as e-books, checklists, or exclusive content, to

encourage visitors to subscribe to your email list. Develop an email sequence to engage subscribers and provide them with valuable content, including affiliate product recommendations. Use segmentation and personalization to tailor your emails to specific audience segments.

5. Social Media Presence: Establish a strong presence on relevant social media platforms where your target audience spends their time. Create engaging profiles and regularly share valuable content, including blog posts, product reviews, or informative videos. Engage with your followers, respond to comments, and participate in relevant discussions. Leverage social media to drive traffic to your website and promote your affiliate offers.

6. SEO Optimization: Implement search engine optimization (SEO) techniques to improve your website's visibility in search engine results. Conduct keyword research to identify relevant keywords and integrate them strategically into

your content. Optimize your meta tags, headings, and image alt tags. Build quality backlinks through guest posting, collaborations, or participating in industry forums to boost your website's authority.

7. Affiliate Network Accounts: Join reputable affiliate networks that align with your niche and target audience. Create accounts and profiles on these networks, ensuring that your information is accurate and up to date. Familiarize yourself with the platform's terms and conditions, commission structures, and available reporting and tracking tools. Research and apply to individual affiliate programs within these networks that resonate with your niche and audience.

8. Tracking and Analytics: Implement tracking and analytics tools to measure the performance of your affiliate marketing efforts. Set up conversion tracking to monitor clicks, conversions, and revenue generated from your affiliate links. Utilize Google Analytics or other web analytics platforms to gain insights into your website traffic, user behavior, and

sources of conversions. Regularly review your data to identify areas for improvement and optimization. Setting up these affiliate marketing assets will provide you with a solid foundation for your journey. Focus on creating valuable content, optimizing your website for search engines, and building a strong online presence. Leverage email marketing and social media to engage with your audience and promote your affiliate offers. Track your performance through analytics and continuously refine your strategies based on data-driven insights.

18.3 LAUNCHING YOUR FIRST AFFILIATE MARKETING CAMPAIGN

Launching your first affiliate marketing campaign is an exciting step towards earning revenue and building your online presence. Here's a step-by-step guide to help you successfully launch your first affiliate marketing campaign:

1. **Define Your Campaign Objective:** Determine the objective of your campaign, whether it's to drive sales, generate leads, increase brand awareness, or promote a specific product

or service. Having a clear objective will guide your campaign strategy and help you measure its success.

2. Select Relevant Affiliate Products: Choose affiliate products or services that align with your target audience's interests and needs. Research and select high-quality products from reputable merchants that you genuinely believe in and can confidently promote to your audience.

3. Craft Compelling Campaign Content: Create compelling content that educates, informs, and persuades your audience to take action. This can include product reviews, comparison articles, tutorials, or engaging social media posts. Focus on the benefits, features, and unique selling points of the affiliate products you're promoting.

4. Incorporate Affiliate Links Strategically: Strategically place your affiliate links within your content to maximize visibility and click-through rates. Use anchor texts, call-to-action buttons, or custom banners that seamlessly integrate with your content. Make sure your affiliate links are properly

tracked using unique identifiers provided by the affiliate program.

5. Optimize Landing Pages: If you're directing traffic to dedicated landing pages, optimize them for conversions. Ensure clear and compelling messaging, prominent call-to-action buttons, and a user-friendly layout. Implement tracking pixels or codes to measure the performance of your landing pages and make data-driven improvements.

6. Promote Your Campaign: Leverage various marketing channels to promote your campaign. Share your campaign content on your website, blog, social media platforms, and email newsletters. Consider guest posting on relevant blogs, collaborating with influencers, or participating in industry forums to expand your reach and drive targeted traffic to your campaign.

7. Track and Measure Performance: Utilize tracking and analytics tools to monitor the performance of your campaign.

Track clicks, conversions, and revenue generated from your affiliate links. Analyze data such as traffic sources, conversion rates, and engagement metrics to identify areas for optimization and improvement.

8. Engage with Your Audience: Engage with your audience throughout your campaign. Respond to comments, answer questions, and provide additional information or support when needed. Foster a sense of trust and reliability by being accessible and attentive to your audience's needs.

9. Analyze Results and Optimize: Regularly analyze the results of your campaign using the data collected. Identify what's working well and areas that need improvement. Adjust your strategies, content, or promotional tactics based on the insights gained. Continuously optimize and refine your campaign to maximize its effectiveness.

10. Evaluate and Learn: After your campaign has ended, evaluate its overall performance and success.

Review the achieved objectives, revenue generated, audience engagement, and lessons learned. Apply these insights to future campaigns to refine your strategies and improve your results. By following these steps, you'll be able to successfully launch your first affiliate marketing campaign. Remember to provide value to your audience, choose relevant products, optimize your content and landing pages, promote your campaign effectively, track and measure your performance, and continuously refine your strategies based on data-driven insights.

18.4 EVALUATING AND ADJUSTING YOUR PLAN AFTER 90 DAYS

After the initial 90 days of your affiliate marketing journey, it's crucial to evaluate your progress and make necessary adjustments. Here are the steps to effectively evaluate and adjust your plan:

1. **Review Your Goals:** Reflect on the goals you set at the beginning of your affiliate marketing journey. Evaluate how well you have achieved them during the first 90 days.

Determine if any adjustments need to be made to your goals based on your current progress and insights gained.

2. Analyze Performance Metrics: Review the performance metrics and data collected during the first 90 days. Examine key indicators such as website traffic, conversion rates, revenue generated, engagement levels, and audience growth. Identify patterns, trends, and areas for improvement.

3. Identify Successful Strategies: Identify the strategies that have yielded positive results during the initial phase of your affiliate marketing journey. Determine which promotional channels, content types, or marketing tactics have driven the most traffic, conversions, or revenue. Recognize the strengths and successes to build upon in the future.

4. Identify Areas for Improvement: Identify areas where your performance may have fallen short or opportunities for improvement. Analyze data to understand potential bottlenecks or factors contributing to lower conversion rates or

engagement. Look for ways to optimize your content, promotional efforts, or user experience based on these insights.

5. Seek Feedback from Your Audience: Engage with your audience to gather feedback on their experience with your content and affiliate recommendations. Encourage them to share their thoughts, suggestions, and pain points. This feedback can provide valuable insights for refining your strategies and better meeting your audience's needs.

6. Adjust Your Content Strategy: Based on the insights gained, adjust your content strategy for the upcoming period. Determine if there are content topics or formats that resonated particularly well with your audience. Consider incorporating new content types or exploring different angles to further engage your audience.

7. Refine Your Promotional Tactics: Evaluate the effectiveness of your promotional tactics and channels. Determine if certain platforms or campaigns have yielded

better results than others. Adjust your promotional efforts by focusing more on the strategies that have shown promising outcomes and exploring new avenues for reaching your target audience.

8. Assess Affiliate Program Performance: Review the performance of the affiliate programs you have been promoting. Consider factors such as commission rates, conversion rates, payment reliability, and affiliate support. Assess if the programs align well with your audience and if they have met your expectations in terms of revenue generation.

9. Set New Goals and Milestones: Based on your evaluation and adjustments, set new goals and milestones for the next phase of your affiliate marketing journey. Ensure that these goals are realistic, measurable, and align with your long-term vision. Establish a timeline and action plan to guide your efforts moving forward.

10. Continuously Learn and Adapt: Maintain a mindset of continuous learning and adaptation. Stay updated with

industry trends, algorithm changes, and new marketing strategies. Engage in professional development opportunities, join affiliate marketing communities, and seek mentorship or guidance when needed. Adapt your strategies based on feedback, market trends, and data analysis to enhance your performance. By evaluating your progress, making necessary adjustments, and setting new goals, you can ensure ongoing growth and success in your affiliate marketing journey. Continuously monitor performance, stay connected with your audience, and adapt your strategies based on feedback and data-driven insights. Embrace the iterative nature of affiliate marketing, and always be open to learning and adapting to the ever-changing landscape of the industry.

In this book, we have explored the world of affiliate marketing, providing beginners with valuable insights and practical guidance. We have covered the essential topics and strategies necessary for starting a successful affiliate marketing journey. From understanding the fundamentals of affiliate marketing to building your platform, selecting niches, choosing affiliate programs, and implementing various marketing techniques, we have aimed to equip you with the knowledge and tools needed to thrive in this industry. Throughout this book, we emphasized the importance of setting clear goals, understanding your target audience, creating valuable content, and building trust and credibility with your audience. We discussed the significance of leveraging various marketing channels, such as SEO, social media, email marketing, and paid advertising, to drive traffic to your affiliate links. We also explored advanced strategies, such as sales funnels, retargeting, and automation, to scale your affiliate business and increase conversions.

We highlighted the role of technology, including AI, machine learning, big data, and blockchain, in shaping the future of affiliate marketing. We emphasized the need to adapt to industry changes, stay informed about emerging trends, and continuously learn and refine your strategies to stay ahead of the competition. As you embark on your affiliate marketing journey, remember that success in this field requires patience, dedication, and continuous learning. Keep track of your performance metrics, analyze the data, and make adjustments based on insights gained. Cultivate strong relationships with affiliate networks, merchants, influencers, and your audience to foster growth and collaboration. Affiliate marketing is a dynamic and ever-evolving industry, offering immense opportunities for those who are willing to put in the effort. As you apply the knowledge gained from this book, be creative, experiment, and find your unique voice and approach within the affiliate marketing landscape.

Remember, the key to success lies in providing value to your audience, promoting products and services you genuinely believe in, and always maintaining transparency and honesty in your marketing efforts. We hope this book has provided you with a solid foundation to start your affiliate marketing journey and inspired you to pursue this exciting and lucrative path. As you move forward, embrace the challenges, stay adaptable, and never stop learning and growing.

Best of luck in your affiliate marketing endeavors!

Dear Reader,

Thank you for choosing to read "Affiliate Marketing for Beginners 2023." We would like to express our sincere gratitude for your support and for investing your time and trust in this book. We hope that the knowledge and insights you have gained from these pages will empower you to embark on a successful affiliate marketing journey. If you found this book valuable and informative, we kindly ask you to consider leaving a positive review on the platform where you purchased or read it. Your feedback will not only help us understand how we can improve but will also assist others in making an informed decision when choosing resources to begin their own affiliate marketing journey. Thank you once again for your support. We wish you great success as you embark on your affiliate marketing endeavors!

ALBERT IRVIN

Made in the USA
Middletown, DE
05 August 2023

36214757R00126